Beside Still Waters

Great Prayers of the Bible for Today

By Marlene Chase

Copyright 2005 The Salvation Army

Published by Crest Books, Salvation Army National Headquarters
615 Slaters Lane, Alexandria, Virginia 22314
(703) 684-5518 Fax: (703) 684-5539
http: //www.salvationarmyusa.org

Printed in the United States of America

Photographs including cover by Diane E. Tolcher

Book design and layout by Bremmer & Goris

Library of Congress Catalog Card Number: 2005932920

ISBN 0-9740940-6-4

Dedicated to the readers, writers, staff and friends of the USA War Cry who have encouraged and uplifted me during the years I have been privileged to serve as editor in chief for the Salvation Army's National Publications. "In all my prayers for all of you, I always pray with joy because of your partnership in the gospel" (Phil. 1:3).

CONTENTS

"Come to the Waters—Poems of Inspiration" follows page 56.

Preface

What we believe about prayer depends largely on our understanding of God and what we have been taught to believe about Him. Not everyone is lucky enough to have had a parent or a mentor who encouraged childhood prayer to a loving God who is powerful and good and who hears and responds to those who call on Him.

We may have been taught to pray at each meal and before bed, a discipline that established a pattern for later understanding and faith, but there is much more to learn about communication with God. Each day brings new discoveries, for His "mercies are new every morning" (Lam. 3:23). Prayer is both journey and destination, yearning and fulfillment. Its mysteries are deep enough to keep us seeking for a lifetime the closer company of God—what prayer is all about. "To the thirsty I will give from the fountain of the water of life without payment," Jesus said (Rev. 2:16).

Prayer has sustained men and women of faith since the beginning of time, bringing hope to the hopeless and making of the desert a blossoming garden. Prayer has changed the course of history and made saints of sinners. Its direct connection can be traced to events that have changed the world, such as the establishment of missions over the centuries, the demise of slavery in the nineteenth century and the fall of the Berlin Wall in recent times.

The Salvation Army has since its beginning placed a consistent and prominent emphasis on prayer. William Booth, who in 1903 was invited to open the United States Senate with an invocation to God, urged those who signed the membership card of the Christian Mission (early name for The Salvation Army) to "pray believingly, live holily and labor earnestly." He declared that as long as Salvationists did this, they would have success in winning souls.

While the old term for prayer, "knee drill," has been replaced with "prayer meeting," none of the import and power of this Christian act of worship and survival has changed for the Army or the Church universal. We still believe that "prayer is the Christian's native air, his vital breath" (James Montgomery), and that it is necessary for continued progress in the individual Christian life and in the corporate body of Christ. Yet, we find ourselves more and more uncomfortable as we see the number of prayer meetings decline and the crowd of pray-ers diminish. What other meeting on some church calendars could accommodate its attenders in a room the size of a broom closet?

Some congregations have abandoned the prayer meeting altogether, sometimes putting in its place a Bible study with the last five minutes of the hour reserved for the prayers of the faithful who will participate. Is it enough? Perhaps. After all, we're still alive—even growing in certain ways. And we still find it possible to carry out one part of the Founder's three-fold injunction. We still "labor earnestly." But is it possible to live holy lives without consistent, believing prayer? And how certain is our success in winning souls without it?

Christians will lose their way and our churches will die without prayer. We need to take fresh hold of its principles as a drowning man grasps a life preserver. If our fingers have slipped off in the past, we must not give up. God continues to throw out the life preserver of prayer, waiting with longing for His loved ones to seek His face.

It's time to consider again that Jesus, who taught His disciples to pray, could not go a day without meeting His Father in fervent, loving prayer. And we must ask ourselves why He who needed to pray so little prayed so much when we, who need to pray so much, pray so little.

Human society was meant to be a covenant between God and humankind, a collaborative enterprise based on common values and vision. But we are blown by prevailing winds in a culture that has made man the center of all things and chosen its own small gods. Only a determined will to persevere in fellowship with God and His saints will keep us morally upright in an age of immoral pressures.

We keep our terms of this covenant called life through communion with God. We believe that He is the central locus of morality and of our individual lives, that He is the One who creates and sustains us. God is the Designer of life, its Source and its Object; we make contact with Him through prayer.

Though we can learn much about prayer from God's Word and from putting into practice the steps intrinsic to it, prayer is at its core mystery, even as God is mystery. We simply cannot put God in a box and know precisely how He operates. If we could, He would be like us and unworthy of worship.

He is God—infinitely higher than we are. The Psalmist in hyperbole wrote, "His ways are past finding out!" The Incarnation, which revealed

Jesus as the express image of God, helps us to know much more about those ways, but it should always be in the deepest spirit of humility that we approach God and seek to live in Him.

"The glorious riches of this mystery (is) Christ in you, the hope of Glory" (Col. 1:27). What great mystery, what grace, that the God of the universe, who spoke whole worlds into existence, desires our company. Though it defies complete understanding in our limited state, we accept the gift of Himself in childlike faith. "Now as always, God discloses Himself to 'babes' and hides Himself in thick darkness from the wise and prudent. We must simplify our approach to Him. We must strip down to essentials (and they will be found to be blessedly few). We must put away all effort to impress, and come with the guileless candor of childhood. If we do this, without doubt God will quickly respond" (A.W. Tozer in *The Pursuit of God*).

It is always this matter of human pride that separates us from God. Atomic physicist Fredrich Dessauer wrote, "Man is a creature who depends entirely on revelation. In all his intellectual endeavor, he should always listen, always be intent to hear and see. He should not strive to superimpose the structures of his own mind, his systems of thought upon reality. At the beginning of all spiritual endeavor stands humility, and he who loses it can achieve no other heights than the heights of disillusionment."

We can trust God because He not only designed us and knows all about us, but He loves us. As Blaisé Pascal put it, "Jesus Christ is a God whom we approach without pride, and before whom we humble ourselves without despair." God calls us to Himself because He longs to have fellowship with us. That is what prayer is, a pressing in toward the divine center to meet with God.

From the very beginning, God established communication with His creatures. He looked for Adam in the cool of the garden. "The Lord spoke to Moses face to face as a man speaks with his friend" (Exod. 33:11). God invited the Hebrew believers to include Him in every detail of their lives. Together they carried on conversation about the daily stuff of living. Though many of their prayers were self-centered and sometimes unwise, they learned "other centeredness" through the reality of simple prayer. As they communed with the Master of the universe they grew in their understanding. They expressed their simple trust in

His power: "You hold me by my right hand," wrote the Psalmist. "You guide me with Your counsel, and afterward you will take me into Your glory" (Psalm 73:24).

We read that Jesus rose early in the day or went to a quiet place to pray. He taught us to "remain in the Father's love" (John 15: 9). We do this through prayer and find power to conquer temptation, even as Jesus drew personal strength to face crucifixion and death (see Luke 22:39-46). He taught us that it is impossible to stay connected to God without prayer. "Without Me, you can do nothing," Jesus said (John 15:5). We may build buildings, amass constituents, assuage physical hunger, produce high tech literature, but we will do nothing of permanence. This is true because prayer puts us in communication, not with techniques, but with the great Teacher.

Prayer wraps itself around every dimension of life. It moves us upward to the Father, teaching us to embrace Him as Creator, Lord and Guide. It moves us inward to see ourselves in contrast to His majesty as we are drawn to explore the hungers of our souls and to analyze our thoughts and actions. As we seek His face, our personal behavior and goals change until they line up with Jesus' will and way. Prayer moves us outward—beyond ourselves. We commune with the God who loves the world and gives Himself that "whosoever will may be saved" (John 3:16). And we are moved to embrace the world.

We can see these three dimensions—the upward, the inward, and the outward—in the prayers of the men and women of the Bible. As we read and reflect on them, we trace the mystery of fellowship with God and see how it changes lives and affects the little and large events of every day. In the pages that follow, we will explore through Scripture, poetry and water imagery how to commune with our Lord whose life is the living water that springs up into everlasting life and refreshes us daily. Let us learn how best to drink from His unquenchable Spirit.

Moving Upward Through Prayer

Jesus said, "Whoever drinks the water I give him will never thirst. Indeed, the water I give him will become in him a spring of water welling up to eternal life" (John 4:14). Prayer draws us near to the eternal Source of all things, to the One high above all for whom and by whom we were created.

Frederick Buechner writes, "All men pray, even if only through clenched teeth." Many a prayer is unwittingly expressed—hidden in hunger, camouflaged in a curse. Jesus teaches us the glory of true prayer—fellowship with Himself. He teaches us to begin by hallowing the name of God and seeking the divine will.

When we recognize our own unworthiness and look into the face of God's holiness, beauty and unconditional love, faith is ignited. It may be simple faith only as small as a grain of mustard seed, but Jesus told us even that "can move mountains" (Matt. 17:20). So we cast ourselves into the fountain of God's grace and begin the ascent upward in search of Him who alone can satisfy the human spirit.

Chapter 1

LIVING PRAYER

Our Father, which art in heaven. Hallowed be Your Name.
Your Kingdom come, Your will be done on earth as it is in
Heaven. Give us this day our daily bread, and forgive
us our debts as we forgive our debtors. And lead us not
into temptation, but deliver us from evil. For Yours is the
Kingdom, the power and the glory forever. Amen.

Jesus' model prayer in Matthew 6 is one of brevity and simplicity. It can be spoken in less than 30 seconds, but its import reaches deep into the human psyche and covers the depths of the personality. The words we speak in prayer are the outward expression of inward grace that God works in us as we listen to Him and abide in Him.

Attitudes of mind and heart are intrinsic to the Lord's Prayer, reflecting lives that please God and that embody the intent of the prayer. We do not so much "speak" prayer as live it, so that our lives are themselves prayers.

Community

This is a prayer for the whole family of believers. We begin by addressing Him as "Our Father." "Our" underscores that we live in community, not on some island of personal isolation or conceit. We live in the protection and preservation of brother and sisterhood, loving one another deeply and responding to each other's needs.

Christians are members of Christ's body, writes Commissioner Samuel Logan Brengle. "They should be as loving, as forbearing, as sympathetic and helpful toward each other as are my two hands." How different the world would be if we really understood that we are part of the another, as bound to each other as our hands are to the body.

Intimacy

"Father" describes our intimate relationship with Him. "Those who are led by the Spirit of God are sons of God," writes Paul. "You received the Spirit of sonship. And by Him we cry out, 'Abba, Father'" (Rom. 8:14-15).

We come to Him as to a beloved "daddy," which is what the Aramic word, Abba, means. It affirms the most intimate of relationships. More than merely saying "Father," we pour all of our intention and love into living according to His design as obedient children who know their Father intimately.

We grow in intimacy as we walk with Him in obedience. He wants us to experience the joy of really knowing Him so that all the resources of the divine power He holds can be ours.

Reverence

"Hallowed be Your Name." God's name implies His personal presence and power in the life of His children who honor Him as sovereign. We pray for His kingdom to be established, a petition that will not be fulfilled completely until Jesus returns. One day everyone will acknowledge God as Lord, and all sin will be banished. Righteousness will reign, but Christ's Kingdom can reign supremely and completely in our individual lives now. We can allow Him to save us from all sin, and to cooperate with His righteous spirit, so that nothing unholy is allowed to consist with the divine rule. The deepest reverence we can show is to live the prayer, "Your will be done."

Trust

"Give us this day our daily bread." God is concerned about our physical needs as well as our spiritual ones, and we can trust Him to meet them. "My God will meet all your need," writes Paul, "according to His riches in glory by Christ Jesus (Phil. 4:19). He doesn't promise to meet our wants, but our needs. Nor is there any limit to His resources.

An Old Testament prayer by Agur, an obscure saint who is only mentioned once in Scripture, strikes a strong parallel to the Lord's Prayer. "Give me neither poverty nor riches," he wrote, "give me only my daily bread. Otherwise, I may have too much and disown You and say, 'Who is the Lord?' Or I may become poor and steal, and so dishonor the name of my God" (Prov. 30:8-9). This early saint had an amazing understanding of material blessings. He asked for his fair portion, but no more. More leads to pride; less to theft. Earlier in his wise saying, Agur affirmed, "Every word of God is flawless; He is a shield to those who take refuge in Him" (Prov. 30:5).

Forgiveness

"Forgive us our trespasses as we forgive those who trespass against us." Jesus' model prayer speaks to our need to live in an attitude of humility, forgiving those who wrong us. It is a necessary response to the forgiveness of God in our own lives, but it does not earn His forgiveness, which is pure grace—the gift of God.

We are often hard on others, expecting perfection, reluctant to forgive the mistakes they make—especially when we are the ones hurt. He requires that we live in loving acceptance of one another, aware that each of us is subject to weakness and error.

In writing to the Galatians, Paul urged, "If someone is caught in a sin, you who are spiritual should restore him gently, but watch yourself, or you also may be tempted. Carry each other's burdens and in this way you will fulfill the law of Christ" (Gal. 6:1-2). Secularists in the 21st century tout tolerance as the highest virtue, but Jesus taught no such weak substitute. He called us to live by love.

Defense of Faith

"Lead us not into temptation, but deliver us from evil." Matthew 6:13 is a plea that we be kept from straying and losing our faith as a result of trials. God does not lead us into temptation. James reminds us, "Let no one say when he is tempted, 'I am tempted by God; for God cannot be tempted by evil, nor does He Himself tempt anyone. But each one is tempted when he is drawn away by his own desires and enticed. Then when desire has conceived, it gives birth to sin; and sin, when it is full-grown, brings forth death" (James 1:13-15 NKJV).

Faith is the most precious possession we have. We need to fight for it, to shun sin in all its forms and to "Build (ourselves) up on (our) most holy faith," as Jude the Apostle wrote. God keeps His part of the covenant, but we must "keep (ourselves) in God's love" (Jude 20-21).

Praise and Thanksgiving

"For Yours is the kingdom, the power and the glory forever." The conclusion to Jesus' model prayer calls us to live in the attitude of praise and thanksgiving, honoring God as the Eternal One whose Kingdom is never ending. While scholars believe this ascription was not in the earliest text of the prayer but added for use in public worship, it underscores our need to give thanks and to praise our God. It keeps us mindful of the eternal nature of God's Kingdom and our dependence on Him for every breath.

It is important to pray these words both in public and private prayer and to see that they reflect the attitudes of our hearts. Jesus teaches us to pray by teaching us how to live—in loving community, in intimacy with Him, in reverence, trust, humility and thanksgiving as we guard our most holy faith.

If we had no example of prayer but this one from our Lord Himself, we would have all we need to live as true Christians in this world. No mere rhetoric, Jesus taught living prayer!

Chapter 2

A Prayer of Hunger

"O Lord ... You still the hunger of those you cherish ...

And I—in righteousness I will see Your face; when I awake,

I will be satisfied with seeing Your likeness" (Psalm 17:14-15).

Everyone experiences a longing for God at some time in their life. Like Job, we may even have said aloud, "If only I knew where to find Him; if only I could go to His dwelling!" (23:3): As small children, before we were turned away from God by the apathy or hostility of others or by our own dwindling capacity to believe, we found it quite natural to talk to God, embracing Him as friend or soul mate.

Perhaps this innate tendency to love God and to seek His friendship is one reason why Jesus urged us to imitate children. "Unless you change and become like little children," He said, "you will never enter the kingdom of heaven" (Matt. 18:4).

Disappointment over what we thought God should do about some terrible occurrence in our lives may have distanced us from Him. We who once longed for Him may have turned Him away out of anger or sorrow and dulled our ears to His voice for so long that His whisper is hard to detect. Yet, the persistent ache within testifies that something is amiss.

The great theologian Pascal referred to our longing for God as a vacuum in the soul that cannot be filled with anyone or anything except the God who shaped it. Since God made us in His image and for fellowship with Him, the longing to fulfill that purpose for which we were created accompanies us from our earliest years. We don't always recognize what it is—this homesickness or lovesickness that defies healing. But we know that something inside us is broken and desolate without Him.

Written in the Universe

Paul, speaking to the Romans in the first century A.D., acknowledged that the divine stamp is written in the universe. "Since the creation of the world,

God's invisible qualities—His eternal power and divine nature—have been clearly seen, being understood from what has been made, so that men are without excuse" (Rom. 1:20). He further indicates that "the requirements of the law are written on (our) hearts, (our) consciences also bearing witness" of God's being and presence (2:15).

We cannot write God off, however hurt or disenchanted we have become through events, inadequate perceptions or disappointments at the hands of those who should most closely have resembled Him. We may try to fill the void in our lives with human relationships, with extensive knowledge, engaging pursuits and treasures the earth affords, but in the end, we will find the emptiness still deep, still pervasive.

"Every creature seeks to become like God, writes Meister Eckhart. "Nature's intent is neither food nor drink nor clothing nor comfort nor anything else in which God is left out. Whether you like it or not, whether you know it or not, secretly nature seeks, hunts, tries to ferret out the track on which God may be found."

Written on God's Heart

The happy thing about our human longing for God is that God is equally thirsty for relationship with us. That is the stunning mystery. "What is man that You are mindful of him and the son of man that You care for him?" the Psalmist asked incredulously (Psalm 8:4). The Scripture teaches us that God is love and that He longs for us with great yearning. "As a father has compassion on his children, so the Lord has compassion on those who fear (honor) Him" (Psalm 103:13). Nowhere did He reveal his love more fully than in Jesus Christ, who gave His life to restore us to fellowship with God. When we think of all He has done, it cannot but move us to astonishment that, in spite of His greatness, He cherishes communion with us.

Henri Nouwen tells of three fathers who traveled to visit St. Anthony, the father of monks, every year. Two of them would discuss their thoughts and the salvation of their souls with St. Anthony, but a third remained silent and did not ask him anything. After a long time St. Anthony said to him, "You often come here to see me, but you never ask me anything." The other replied, "It is enough to see you, Father."

The Psalmist's prayer echoes this desire for holy fellowship. "O Lord ... You still the hunger of those you cherish ... And I—in righteousness I will see Your face; ... I will be satisfied with seeing Your likeness" (Psalm 17:14-15).

We are sometimes blinded by our wants, deafened by the sound of our own voices, but our real need is for fellowship—to simply be with Him. And His joy is to meet with us.

The Family Likeness

Yearning for God is tied to our likeness to Him. Created by Him and for Him, we realize that we will never be whole and happy apart from Him. Spending time with God develops the family likeness in us. When I travel where people know my daughters, I often hear expressions like, "Well, you certainly can't deny your children. They look just like you!" Or "Your daughter has the same way of smiling—something in the eyes ..." It's more than just the bloodline, though, that informs this likeness. It has to do with our being together in close company day after day through the give and take of life that makes the bond recognizable.

We have an inborn likeness to God. His stamp is on us, for we are made in His image. Yet, another stamp has been superimposed because of sin, which renders us powerless against spiritual enemies and distances us from the One who loves us with an everlasting love. Oh, that our daily prayer would be "Let me see You, Lord and awake satisfied with seeing Your likeness in me." Such communion with our Lord satisfies our longing and brings delight, a joy that John Pierre Caussade describes as being "light as a feather, fluid as water, innocent as a child responding to the grace of God like a floating balloon."

Yes, our hunger for Him is natural, and He understands our desperate need for Him. He listens and will surely respond in His way and time. We can be confident that the cry of our hearts falls on the most loving ear.

Chapter 3

PRAYER TO THE GOD OF ALL KNOWING

"O Lord, You have searched me and You know me. You
know when I sit and when I rise; You perceive my thoughts
from afar. You discern my going out and my lying down;
You are familiar with all my ways" (Psalm 139:1-3).

The psalms and prayers of David always begin with the conviction that
God knows everything about him and about everyone and everything
else in the world. And down through the centuries we too have affirmed
that truth about God—even though we often pray and live in ways
contrary to our dogma.

Sometimes we go to great lengths to describe a situation to God, to
inform Him, as it were, of the facts in our case. Sometimes in great stress
or discouragement we question if He has any idea of the agony we're
going through. Sometimes we wonder if He really is there at all. We who
live in the great cloud of unknowing find it difficult to imagine that any
being lives above that cloud.

The Cloud of Unknowing

"It's easier for me to believe in a God who doesn't know everything,"
says a friend of mine. "It's easier than believing that He knows the
terrible thing beating me down but doesn't move to help me." She
speaks out of the great cloud of unknowing—the cloud of temporal life
that parades as the be–all, end–all of existence.

In the fourteenth century an unknown mystic wrote a treatise called
The Cloud of Unknowing. The cloud is the gulf between man and God, and
the text discusses how to bridge that gulf. Considered one of the finest works
of the Middle English mystical tradition, the book teaches that love of God
and the denial of self will make it possible to experience Him.

Though archaic language might obscure the perennial truth
contained in this classic work about prayer, it echoes Scripture's teaching
that God invites us to come to Him in simple faith, believing that He

hears and cares. "A little word of one syllable when it is not only spoken or thought, but privily meant in the deepness of spirit ... pierceth the ears of Almighty God (more) than doth any long psalter unmindfully mumbled in the teeth."

Jesus told us that God knows what we need even before we ask, and urges the believer committed to His will, "If you ask anything in My name, I will do it" (John 14:14). But how can this be? How can we approach a holy, omniscient God?

"Without faith it is impossible to please Him" (Heb. 11:6). Only God can give us the faith to trust when we do not understand and to believe when we do not see. Sometimes what we perceive as hurtful and harsh works to our benefit. Only faith in a God who knows and cares can circumvent the cloud of unknowing that surrounds us in the daily give and take of life. "For I tell thee truly," writes the 14th century saint, "that ofttimes patience in sickness and in other diverse tribulations pleaseth God much more than any liking devotion that thou mayest have in thy health."

We were not made for this life only but for eternity. Jesus said, "Do not worry, saying, 'What shall we eat?' or 'What shall we drink?' or 'What shall we wear?' ... For your heavenly Father knows that you need them. But seek first His kingdom and His righteousness, and all these things will be given to you as well" (Matt 6:31-33).

Piercing the Cloud

"God is Spirit, and His worshippers must worship in spirit and in truth" (John 4:24). Does this mean that God has no interest in things that relate to the body, only in what relates to our spirit? But isn't He the one who turned water into wine at a wedding, who made sure a widow's oil wouldn't run out? Didn't He care for a petulant, conniving woman and her son when they were turned out of Abraham's house?

Does He care about the things that our lives are made up of? Food and health and family? Some believers in the early church came to a false conclusion that He does not. They were called Gnostics and circulated a rumor that all flesh was evil and only spirit was good. They couldn't get their minds around the mystical union of flesh and spirit, so they endeavored to bring God down to their level. It's a mistake many have made and one that is perpetuated in different guises today.

Before we write the Gostics off as incapable of deep thought, we should be aware of our own tendency to make God over into a simpler image that everyone can understand. When some inexplicable event occurs that defies easy interpretation, do we hastily ascribe an intention on the part of the Almighty that fits with our limited understanding of righteousness?

When a child dies, do we try to assuage the grief of a friend by the notion that God needed another angel in heaven? When a whole village is wiped out by disaster, do we accept it as the judgment of God for evil doing? When everything is working to our advantage, do we assume God is pleased with us?

God is greater than our human understanding, deeper than our studied intelligence, wider than the scope of science or art or religion. He is the eternal, all knowing God. "Can you fathom the mysteries of God? Can you probe the limits of the Almighty? They are higher than the heavens—what can you do? They are deeper than the depths of the grave—what can you know? Their measure is longer than the earth and wider than the sea" (Job 11:7-10).

Only faith can pierce the cloud of unknowing. Faith in the One who knows all about us and loves us still. The author of *The Cloud of Unknowing* wrote, "It is that a soul hath comprehended after the lesson of Saint Paul ... the length and the breadth, the height and the deepness of everlasting and all–lovely, almighty, and all–witting God. The everlastingness of God is His length. His love is His breadth. His might is His height. And His wisdom is His deepness."

Such knowing is not of our own making. It is God who gives to each of us a measure of faith and waits to broaden and heighten and deepen that understanding as we embrace Him in love. "By faith we understand ..." all things (Heb. 11:3), and such wisdom is priceless and eternal. "If any of you lacks wisdom," God says through the Apostle James, "he should ask God" (1:5).

There it is. We are thrown back upon the eternal One, the God of all knowing who makes Himself known through love as we live in humble, searching faith. It begins with Him. It ends with Him. It always has; it always will.

Chapter 4

PRAYER OF REMEMBRANCE

*"O Lord, let Your ear be attentive to the prayer of this
Your servant and to the prayer of Your servants who
delight in revering Your name.... Grant him favor"*
(Neh. 1:11).

One of the Bible's great prayers was given in the year 445 B.C., by a
cupbearer to King Artaxerxes in the Persian empire (southern Iran near
the Persian Gulf). Nehemiah, whose name means "The Lord Comforts,"
had been among the exiles returning home to Jerusalem from captivity
in Babylon, after King Cyrus released them. The Jews faced many
problems in the aftermath of the decree. Chief among them was how to
maintain their distinctive heritage, for they were a powerless, subject
people in an empire whose rulers did not view the God of their forefa-
thers as the one true God. He was one god among many. All religious
beliefs were merged into one, and while each group was encouraged to
maintain its distinctive heritage, they had to do so without exclusivity.
It was understood that all roads lead to heaven and no one could claim
theirs to be the only way.

Endangered Species

The temptation was to gradually acquiesce to the prevailing mores of
society and to assimilate the surrounding pagan cultures. They might
preserve some of their customs with careful initiative, but they were
in danger of surrendering the God-given theology, which had been
entrusted to them. Nehemiah was one of five men who kept intact
the Jews' identity, showing that they were to be a nation of priests,
serving God and declaring Him before the world. They accomplished
this in spite of hostile neighbors and physical challenges, but only
through reliance on the providence of God. They learned the wisdom of
obedience, the importance of distinctness of belief and separation from
wordly practices through prayer.

Each of us has a spiritual heritage. It is not the purview of one privileged nation or group of people. Each of us is made in the image of God, and it is the whole duty of mankind to "act justly and to love mercy and to walk humbly with" Him (Micah 6:8). We do not need to look far to see that we have failed rather miserably to project the image of our heavenly Father in present-day society. Polls indicate that the rate of divorce in the church is on par with that of society at large, and reports of fraud, embezzlement, sexual abuse and other sins dog our steps. We should be driven to our knees in the kind of personal and corporate confession that leads to restoration.

Looking in the Right Place

What is really at issue when we pray is how we understand God. Is He a distant figure in the sky who whimsically answers a prayer here and there if it pleases Him? Is He merely the divine spark within us, so that praying is little more than talking to ourselves, a projection of our own desires? Or is He the holy, awesome "Other" who is to be worshipped both in word and in deed, whose imprimatur can be marked in nature and in the hearts of people?

"Anyone who comes to Him (God) must believe that He exists and that He rewards those who earnestly seek Him" (Heb. 11:6). If you are caught up in the error that mankind simply evolved from a lower life form or that he is some kind of cosmic accident, left now to make his way as best as he can through a disturbing and destructive world, you have little hope of achieving anything in prayer.

The writer to the Hebrews declares that "By faith we understand that the universe was formed at God's command, so that what is seen was not made out of what was visible" (11:3). To pray rightly demands that we know who it is we are speaking to and who is speaking to us. We must look in the right place—not to some saint who lived a good life or to some ethereal representation of God, but to God Himself through Jesus, His Son. "For there is one God and one mediator between God and men, the man Christ Jesus," Paul declares in 1 Timothy 2:5. In spite of prevailing doctrines in our culture today, "Every knee (will) bow ... and every tongue confess that Jesus Christ is Lord, to the glory of God the Father" (Phil 2:10-11). Salvation is found only in Jesus.

Recognizing our Condition

When Nehemiah learned from his countryman, Hanani, that the survivors of the captivity were in great distress and that the walls of Jerusalem had been broken down and its gates burned, he "sat down and wept, and mourned, fasted and prayed before the God of heaven" (1:4). Realizing that the distinctive religion of his people might not survive, he went to the Source of that distinctive belief, indeed to the Source of all life, with his deep concern.

We Christians are also in danger of losing what God has meant for us to experience and to enjoy. Alternatives to godly living abound, some of which sound engaging, practical and scientific. We do well to remember the Psalmist's words, "There is a way that seems right to a man, but in the end it leads to death" (Prov. 14:12). Nehemiah reminds us of the vital need to remember our spiritual heritage, to admit our failure as Nehemiah did on behalf of his people. "We have acted very wickedly toward You. We have not obeyed the commands, decrees and laws You gave your servant Moses" (1:7). After the confession came the appeal: "O Lord, let your ear be attentive to the prayer of this Your servant and to the prayer of Your servants who delight in revering Your name ... grant him favor" (1:11).

Here is our starting place in the consideration of prayer. We must recognize who God is and that He has given us a spiritual heritage to cherish, protect and keep intact for this generation and the next. Our eternal destiny is at stake. "What good is it for a man to gain the whole world, yet forfeit his soul?" Jesus asks in Mark 8:36. "Or what can a man give in exchange for his soul? If anyone is ashamed of Me and My words in this adulterous and sinful generation, the Son of Man will be ashamed of Him when He comes in His Father's glory with the holy angels" (Mark 8:37-38).

Chapter 5

PRAYER AS HOMECOMING

"But the tax collector stood at a distance. He would not
even look up to heaven, but beat his breast and said,
'God, have mercy on me, a sinner'" (Luke 18:13).

The day the biblical tax collector came home to God may have been a
day like any other in Jerusalem. Mules and camels balked as merchants
unloaded their wares in the teeming marketplace. Women shouted,
haggled, pushed and scrambled among the vegetable tables and linen
stalls. Children darted among colorful booths, laughing, hiding,
snatching an unguarded fig or pomegranate.

The men, on their way to the Temple for the daily ritual prayers,
shuffled absently, perhaps thinking of the goods they would sell that day.
Some looked solemn, full of duty. Beggars leaned forward eagerly, hoping
a coin would be tossed their way.

One man, moving alone, saw all this as if in a moment of epiphany. He
kept his head down, for if people recognized him they would step
away in disgust. In Jerusalem, the tax collector was the most despised of
all men—looked upon as a thief, the lowest of the low.

On sudden impulse, he lifted his face for the next passerby. He
would take their full look of wrath. Would to God it could cleanse his
conscience! He watched the finest citizens of the city striding with arms
folded across their long tunics. At the bottom of their robes fringes
swayed and danced to remind the wearers of the commandments. The
longer fringes worn by the Pharisees slapped against the man's legs like
a curse.

He hesitated a step. It had been some time since he had given
thought to the commandments he had memorized so faithfully as a boy.
Why was he thinking of them today at the hour of prayer? He hadn't
meant to be here. He walked on, propelled by something he couldn't
name. Perhaps it was true that all people pray without thinking—the
broken fragments uttered and the poor crippled prayers hidden in minor

blasphemies. Even those who thought God was dead still had to talk to Him, if only through clenched teeth!

Why was he feeling this inexplicable homesickness for the God he had once known?

The Pharisees lifted their arms as they neared the Temple, and the man could see the little parchment scrolls bound on their wrists and foreheads. Phylacteries, the Jews called them. Preservatives, on which were fragments of the Law—charms to preserve them from danger. They took literally the command "Tie them as symbols on your hands and bind them on your foreheads" (Deut. 6:8).

As the publican stared at the little scrolls, the words seemed to burn into his brain, searing his soul. He had not worn the scrolls on his forehead or in his heart. He knew the commandments: love the Lord your God with all your soul, honor your father and mother, remember the Sabbath. The commandments ... For years he had wanted to forget them, to live as he wished, to go his own way. Now he could not stop the words burned into his memory.

The chanting grew louder. He halted. He could not approach the holy place. Maybe the Pharisees could go, speaking their loud prayers, swishing their long-fringed robes, nodding their heads with the little scrolls bobbing between their eyes. But he could not. He was not worthy even to lift his eyes to heaven.

Suddenly someone turned in his direction and prayed in a loud voice. "God, I thank You that I am not like other men—robbers, evildoers, adulterers—or even like this tax collector."

The man felt his pulse quicken. His eyeballs throbbed in their sockets. Yes, he was guilty. He had moved far away from God and all that was good. It seemed as though his whole life was opening at its deepest level, that from afar off he could picture home. Home—waiting arms and shared intimacies.

The Pharisee's voice droned on: "I fast twice a week and give a tenth of all I get!"

The publican's heart beat louder. Was it possible for him to come home? Did God wait to love him, to forgive him? The swelling in his soul was like waves breaking against the shore. He dropped his head on his chest and whispered, "God, have mercy on me, a sinner!" He beat his fists on his chest. It was the symbol for being struck dead and the punishment he knew he deserved.

It seemed an eternity was in the moment. How long he stood in the shadow of the Temple he couldn't have told. Nor could he tell in what second he experienced the beautiful sense of coming home. Stunned by a peace that the noisy world around him could neither disturb or understand the tax collector knew he had crossed over the threshold of home.

Slowly but jubilantly, he moved toward the Temple, eager to enter the sanctuary and praise and adoration to Jehovah whom he had so long ignored ... And it seemed to him that he could almost smell the aroma of fresh bread and the fragrance of the sweet wine. He was coming home.

Confession and penitence make up the threshold of prayer. Humbling ourselves before Him and confessing our sins is how we enter into prayer. Adoration (of God and His forgiving love) is prayer's sanctuary; the presence, vision and enjoyment of God are its bread and wine.

Are you experiencing His presence in your life? Is prayer as real as bread and wine? God longs to share His secrets with us as He did with biblical saints and thousands of the faithful since the beginning of time.

"Seek the Lord while He may be found;
call upon Him while He is near.
Let the wicked forsake his way
and the evil man his thoughts.
Let him turn to the Lord, and He will have mercy upon him,
and to our God, for He will freely pardon" (Isa. 55:6-7).

Chapter 6

Prayer as Thanksgiving

"Always giving thanks to God the Father for everything"

(Eph. 5:20).

Tony Campolo, well-known author and educator, recalls how his son came into the family's living room and announced, "I'm going to pray now. Anybody want anything?"

As a child, I had rather a poor idea of God. I thought of Him as someone who existed just to respond to me, to give me the things I wanted and needed. That's not so terrible. Children view Mom and Dad in very much the same way, believing themselves to be the center of the universe, with everything revolving around them.

It takes time to learn that the world is not created for us alone, and that some of our wants are not good for us. We learn that good parents will not give them. God understands our naiveté about faith. His Word teaches us who He is and gives us the right concept of prayer. We begin with thanksgiving and praise.

Prayer must first bring us to our knees before Him who deserves all our worship. How quickly we forget that God is the ultimate giver of all things. "Every good and perfect gift is from above, coming down from the Father of the heavenly lights, who does not change like shifting shadows" (Jas. 1:17). How He loves to give us joy, to give us Himself. He wants to hear our requests and to give us good things, but He longs more than all for our fellowship, and for us to approach Him in the spirit of worship. Our response to His gracious invitation must be thanksgiving and adoration.

Adoration is the spontaneous yearning of the heart to worship, honor, magnify and bless God. In adoration we forget ourselves, we ask for nothing but to cherish Him. We focus on His goodness and thank Him for being for who He is. Music or a beautiful scene that surprises us and makes us aware of God can stimulate us to give praise, but most often, we are drawn by some inner restlessness, by a longing for God. And knowing that we are looking for Him, He is eager to give us some sense of Himself. He loves to give us good gifts.

"If you, then, though you are evil, know how to give good gifts to your children, how much more will your Father in heaven give good gifts to those who ask Him"(Matt. 7:11)! (His goodness is so great that our goodness seems by contrast evil.) God wants to give us what we long for—and our deepest longing is for God Himself.

Thanksgiving and praise are two sides of worship to God. In thanksgiving, we glorify Him for what He has done for us; praise glorifies God for who He is in Himself. Actually, the two weave in and out of one another and become part of a whole. Biblical writers frequently use the words interchangeably and even on top of one another: "I will give you thanks in the great assembly; among the throngs of people I will praise you" (Ps. 35:18) Thanksgiving and praise splash across the experience of all true adoration simultaneously.

The Old Testament world was soaked with the language of thanksgiving. David chose priests to be ministers before the Ark of the Covenant with a singular commission: "to invoke, thank and praise the Lord." Special singers did nothing but sing praises to the Lord (see 1 Chron. 16:4-36). Leviticus also tells us about thank offerings that were a part of the Israelites' worship (see 7:12).

It's hard to find a page of the Psalter that doesn't contain the rhetoric of thanksgiving: "Give thanks to the Lord, for He is good; His love endures forever" (Ps. 106:1), "I will praise You, O Lord, with all my heart" (Ps. 9:1).

Jesus is our example. The signature written across His life was the prayer "I praise You, Father, Lord of heaven and earth" (Luke 10:21). Paul's life, too, reflected the spirit of gratitude: "I thank my God through Jesus Christ for all of you" (Rom 1:8) Biblical witnesses speak with one voice, urging us to give "thanks to God the Father at all times and for everything in the name of our Lord Jesus Christ" (See Eph. 5:20).

Praise lies on a higher plane than thanksgiving. When we give thanks, our thoughts still circle about ourselves to some extent. But in praise our souls ascend to self-forgetting adoration, aware only the majesty and power of God, His grace and redemption.

The Bible, even the ancient law code, is packed with praise. "He is your praise; He is your God" (Deut. 10:21); "Praise the Lord, O my soul. I will praise the Lord all my life; I will sing praises to my God as long as

I live" (Ps. 146:1-2); "I will extol the Lord at all times; His praise will be on my lips" (Ps. 34:1); "He put a new song in my mouth, a hymn of praise to our God" (Ps. 40:3).

The writer to the Hebrews urges us to "continually offer to God a sacrifice of praise—the fruit of lips that confess His name" (Heb. 13:15). And John assures us that praise is the serious business of heaven. "I heard the voice of many angels, numbering thousands upon thousands, and ten thousand times ten thousand. They circled the throne and the living creatures and the elders. In a loud voice they sang: 'Worthy is the Lamb, who was slain to receive power and wealth and wisdom and strength and honor and glory and praise!'"(Rev. 5:11-12).

When we consider who God is and what He has done, it cannot but move us to astonishment that gives way to thanksgiving, then to praise. Yet, in spite of His greatness, He cares about communion with us. "What is man that you are mindful of him and the son of man that you care for him?" David asked incredulously. Scripture teaches us in a variety of ways the truth that He longs for us to live in fellowship with Him.

"Our God is not made of stone," writes Richard Foster. "His heart is the most sensitive and tender of all. No act goes unnoticed, no matter how insignificant or small. A cup of cold water is enough to put tears in the eyes of God. Like the proud mother who is thrilled to receive a wilted bouquet of dandelions from her child, so God celebrates our feeble expressions of gratitude."

Children are good at giving honest praise—another reason why God wants us to become like them. When we grow up, we become internal, preoccupied with ourselves, and praise becomes hard to give, thanks-giving difficult. What will people say if we get all sentimental and gushy, we wonder, and we hold back like misers, afraid that we'll look foolish or weak.

Early in our lives as Salvation Army officers, we had charge of a small congregation of people. Among them was an elderly woman who lived in a nursing home. As a young woman, she had lost all her children in a fire. Later her mental health was compromised. Because she was challenged in this way and had no one to look after her, she ended up among infirm people far more elderly than she. She had few friends and her habitual chatter was a source of irritation to many. Yet she was one of the most happy and outgoing people I have ever met.

One Sunday her chatter seemed especially annoying as we drove to the church service. It had been a difficult week, and I was contending with an ill child. I felt anything but grateful to God; my heart was anything but filled with praise. When we arrived at the building, I came around to open the car door for her, grumbling under my breath because the janitor had not mowed the grass. Dandelions sprouted in yellow profusion all over the ankle high grass. My companion stepped out and paused in mid-sentence. With a blazing smile she threw up her hands. "Oh, look," she exclaimed in delight. "Look what God gave us on the ground."

She taught me to look with new eyes, and I repented of my ungrateful attitude. I needed help learning to thank God for His many gifts, especially those I often walk right over. As the poet has said, "Full many a flower was born to waste its sweetness on a thoughtless world."

Even though we are spiritually challenged, we may find some stepping-stones that will help us regain a spirit of praise and adoration: We can begin in the small daily miracles of ordinary life. We can pay attention to the little, creatures that creep upon the earth, not by studying or analyzing them, but by simply watching.

Annie Dillard in *Pilgrim at Tinker Creek* suggests that we sit back and listen to the sound of the brook, watch the branches of a swaying tree, notice the color, shape and texture of leaves. Listen to the many symphonies and masterpieces in the world—the rustling leaves, the roar of the ocean, the quiver of a rabbit's nose. In time we will begin to experience these tiny pleasures and be able to look beyond them to the Giver. Thanksgiving, praise and adoration will flow naturally in their proper time.

Richard Foster writes about another stepping stone that he suggests recalls "our grateful center." By this he means travelling back mentally to a time and a place when we were free of all the grasping and grabbing, all the pushing and shoving, all the disapproving and dissenting intrusions of life. For Foster it was a fireplace where at night he pulled out the daybed and climbed under the heavy quilts. A few feet away, the crackling fire blazed. Night after night he'd fall asleep, watching the warm yellow glow.

We can also practice gratitude in a very deliberate way. We can develop a habit of giving thanks for the simple gifts that come our way and we can try to live one entire day in utter thanksgiving. Balance every complaint with ten gratitudes, every criticism with ten compliments. Annie Dillard suggests that when we practice gratitude a time will come when we find ourselves saying to God, not "please," but "thank you."

In small ways we can begin to magnify God. The most exaggerated things we can think of will still fall far below what He deserves. Try praying the expressions found in the Psalms: "O glorify the Lord with me; let us exalt His name together" (Psalm 34:3). These and hundreds more give us patterns for praise. In time the words will not only become our own but will also lead us to form our own loving songs of praise. Speak words of indebtedness to God, and these in turn will lead us to acknowledgment, appreciation, gratitude, thanksgiving, praise and adoration. He is worthy of our best efforts. "Oh, come, let us adore Him—Christ the Lord."

Chapter 7

Praying in the Name of Jesus

"The Father will give you whatever you ask in My name"

(John 15:16).

We close our prayers by saying "in Jesus' name." For some this becomes a traditional repetition they scarcely think about. For others the words make up a kind of superstitious formula without which the prayer will not be heard. But of course, praying in the name of Jesus means something quite different. It involves praying in the spirit of Jesus for the things He purposes for us. We hallow His name by relinquishing control of our lives and praying that His divine purposes will be carried out.

In 1 Samuel 2:35, God says, "I will raise up for myself a faithful priest, who will do according to what is in My heart and mind. I will firmly establish his house, and he will minister before My anointed one always."

God's goal is character. Not just any character, but His own character. When we pray in His name, we are praying that in all things His will should be accomplished. We are not called to a career or assignment. We are called to a life of fulfilling the will of God. We need to ask where Jesus is going rather than setting up our own agenda and asking Him to bless it. "For you did not choose Me," He said, "but I have chosen you and appointed you to go and bear fruit—fruit that will last. Then the Father will give you whatever you ask in My name" (John 15:16).

God asks us to travel a road of self-sacrifice, delayed gratification, responsibility and integrity. It is a paradoxical call that leads to ultimate meaning and joy. This was well documented in the life of Jacob.

Jacob was one of the biblical patriarchs whose greatness was achieved through intense personal struggle. He was a clever, deceptive fellow (his name literally means deceiver) from a dysfunctional family, the twin brother of Esau and his mother's favorite. Esau on the other hand was the father's favorite. It's no wonder that trouble resulted in the lives of these two brothers and in generations to follow.

When Jacob tricked his brother out of his birthright, Esau was so angry that he vowed to kill Jacob. With his mother's help Jacob escaped and began his journey to Haran. An ambitious, talented guy, he had great dreams. But he found himself running for his life in the wilderness. God was his very last thought.

But that is just when God showed up. *"Surprise, Jacob! You haven't given me a single thought, but I care about you and I have a great plan for your life."* He outlined it for Jacob, first identifying Himself. *"I am the Lord, the God of your father Abraham and the God of Isaac. I will give you and your descendants the land on which you are lying ... I am with you and will watch over you wherever you go, and I will bring you back to this land. I will not leave you until I have done what I have promised you"*(Gen. 28:13-15).

That's what's so surprising and exciting about God. Even when we couldn't care less about Him, He pursues us, not because He wants to control us but because He loves us and knows that He can fill our lives with incredible meaning.

At Bethel Jacob had his first encounter with God and it changed his life forever. He made some vows of his own, as most of us do when we first come to God. We pray much as Jacob did—to be preserved from death and for God to be our helper. In return for God's care and protection Jacob promised to embrace his father's God as his own. He even promised to tithe.

But God had much to teach Jacob about life and joy. This was but the beginning of his struggles. He was going in the right direction, but he had not yet recognized the Lord as *his* Lord. He was still referring to Him as "my father's God."

For the next 20 years Jacob learned that walking the narrow way with God was not easy. He ran into Laban, his future father in law, who was equally as conniving and deceitful as he had been. Jacob continued to have difficulty turning over the control of his life until in another place that became holy to Jacob, God met with him again.

Like Jacob, who wanted to follow God but who wasn't willing to exchange his dreams for God's, we find that it is hard to relinquish our personal will. We'll give Him our money, our time, our worship, even our devotion at times, but our wills? To be completely dependent on God is the hardest thing, but it is the path to pure joy.

The biblical account shows Jacob once again running for his life.

He's out in the wilderness, wondering if he's going to be caught with the household gods of Laban, his father-in-law. And God comes again. God doesn't leave us to our own devices. He knows we're crippled on our own. This time there's a great wrestling match—a match of wills—and Jacob is left with a permanent limp—a sign that he had finally turned over the keys of his life to God.

God kept His promises to Jacob, and He will keep His promises to us. He says, "I am come that you might have life and have it more abundantly" (John 10:10). The fulfillment comes when we are willing to give up our own dreams for His grand and perfect design.

A Life Bent to God's Will

Chiune Sugihara had a dream. He grew up in Japan during the early 1900s and wanted to be an ambassador to Russia. He studied hard, learning seven languages. Steady, conscientious and a capable linguist, he gradually made his way up the bureaucratic ladder. By the late 1930's, he was named the Japanese consulate to Lithuania. Although he was inching closer to his dream, he was still considered a low-level civil servant. But that would change, he knew. He believed that nothing could keep him from his dream.

Through hard work and loyalty, Chiune Sugihara moved closer to his goal. He began work as the Japanese consul in Lithuania, but dreamed about his next promotion—the realization of his lifelong career goal to become the ambassador to Russia. But World War II put a hitch in his plans.

Early one morning in the summer of 1940, Chiune woke up to find a group of people gathered around his house. They were Jews desperate to escape Poland as Hitler's army encroached. It soon became clear that he was their only chance to avoid the death camps. They needed him to issue visas, allowing them to flee across the Baltic Sea to Japan and from there to pursue freedom elsewhere.

Three times he cabled his superiors asking permission to write the visas, and three times he was denied. The Japanese government was aligning itself with Hitler. Chiune faced a difficult decision. Would he stick to his own agenda and pursue his dream, or would he seek to meet the needs of these desperate people? Would he risk his family's safety for the possible freedom of these strangers?

Writing in longhand, Chiune Sugihara began to issue visas for the Jews who sought his help. For 28 days during that summer and with only a few breaks for sleep or food, he wrote visa after visa. At night his wife massaged the cramps out of his hand. Each visa, he knew, would allow a whole family to find freedom.

Eventually the Japanese removed Chiune from his job. Yet even on the train to Berlin, he continued to write visas. He shoved them through the window of the train into the hands of desperate Jews as they ran along beside him.

Upon his return to Japan, Chiune Sugihara was fired from the Japanese Foreign Ministry. He spent his remaining years eking out a living as a lightbulb peddler, selling in seven different languages. He never realized his lifelong dream of becoming an ambassador to Russia.

Years after his death, Chiune Sugihara's family was interviewed by a newspaper. When asked why he had defied his government and written the visas for the Jews, his family told about Chiune's commitment to Jesus Christ whom he had accepted when he was a young man. Years later, when surrounded by the desperate Jews, it was God's still, small voice that he heard. He had no choice but to help, to do whatever he could. His widow, Yukiko, expressed it this way: "It was his character that he was always giving priority to someone else, (to) what they needed."

Chiune's family said that he had found fulfillment and was satisfied with his life, even though he never became ambassador to Russia. By listening to God's call, by choosing the narrow road, Chiune found a deep joy and fulfillment that no position or prestige could bring. He was, his family said, more than just a lightbulb peddler who could sell in seven languages. The 10,000 Jews he saved from extermination, as well as their 40,000 descendants, would no doubt agree.

In Jesus' Name—and Way

God's way is always the best way. It has always been. It always will be. Couple that with the truth that God wills only our joy, our full lives lived with significance and spirit, and you can see the majesty of this great truth. Are we willing to turn over the reins, to limp—signifying complete dependence upon God? No dream, however sweet, can compare with the sweet will of God.

The more time we spend with God, learning about Him, talking to Him, listening to Him, the more our wills are bent to His. He longs to share with us His most intimate secrets. Most of the time when we lament over not knowing what the will of God is in a certain matter, it is because we are not willing to act upon what we already know. We are not willing to subject our own wills to His.

Soren Kierkegaard writes: "If a person does not yield himself completely in prayer, he is not praying, even if he were to stay down on his knees day and night. It is the same here as with a person who is maintaining a connection with a distant friend. If he does not see to it that the letter is addressed properly, it will not be delivered and the connection will not be made, no matter how many letters he writes. Similarly, let the one who prays see to it that the prayer is proper, a yielding of himself in the inner being, because otherwise he is not praying to God. And let the one who prays be scrupulously attentive to this, since no deception is possible here in relation to the Searcher of hearts."

That's the way the prayer of faith works. As we exercise faith, God gives us more. And He helps us to know His heart.

Praying in the name of Jesus means praying in the name and spirit of Jesus. What was His continual prayer to the Father while in His earthly body? What was the perpetual spirit of His prayers? Even as He contemplated the cross with its incredible suffering, He said, "My Father, if it is not possible for this cup to be taken away unless I drink it, may Your will be done" (Matt. 26:42).

Jesus' pattern for us included, "Your will be done on earth as it is in heaven" (Matt. 6:10). Until we are willing to will what He wills, we shall never be effective in prayer—either for our own souls or for others.

Chapter 8

A Prayer of Ambiguity

"Lord, I do believe; help me overcome my unbelief"

(Mark 9:24).

"The God who made the world and everything in it, is the Lord of heaven and earth, and does not live in temples built by hands. And He is not served by human hands, as if He needed anything, because He Himself gives all men life and breath and everything else" (Acts 17:24-25). This One who needs nothing and no one waits in loving anticipation to hear the expressions of our lips and hearts and chooses to work in concert with our prayers.

God has planned a collaborative enterprise for His perfect will to be completed. Prayers are great because God is great—greater than any person or plan, even "greater than our own hearts" (1 John 3:20). "Prayer is a powerful thing," wrote Martin Luther, for God has bound and tied Himself thereto. None can believe how powerful prayer is, and what it is able to effect, but those who have learned it by experience."

Sometimes a great deal of faith might seem evident in a particular prayer; other times, there appears to be little at all. Occasionally, it seems that God speaks even when we are aware of no faith at all. This is why we should often remind ourselves that there is mystery in prayer and in God Himself. It will take a lifetime to explore the depths of the Almighty, and even then we will have only touched the surface. His riches are inexhaustible, His glory beyond our understanding. Two brief prayers help us to focus our thoughts on how prayer and faith work together.

Mark records the story of a blind beggar. "As Jesus and His disciples, together with a large crowd, were leaving the city, a blind man, Bartimaeus (that is, the Son of Timaeus), was sitting by the roadside begging. When he heard that it was Jesus of Nazareth, he began to shout, 'Jesus, Son of David, have mercy on me!'" (10: 46-47). He continued to plead for help in spite of the boisterous crowd that tried to silence him. Jesus heard him above the roar and called for him.

In response to prayer, Jesus immediately healed Bartimaeus, and "he followed Jesus along the road" (52).

Bartimaeus was a vulnerable man—blind and totally without resources. He illustrates the spiritual condition of all of us who have not called upon God to save us. Hear the Lord's words: "You say, 'I am rich; I have acquired wealth and do not need a thing.' But you do not realize that you are wretched, pitiful, poor, blind and naked. ... buy from me gold refined in the fire, so you can become rich; and white clothes to wear, so you can cover your shameful nakedness; and salve to put on your eyes, so you can see" (Rev. 3:17-18).

Without God's divine mercy through Jesus Christ who saves us, we are hopeless, naked in our sins, and unable to see spiritual truth. The good news is that God is eagerly poised to save us, and is calling insistently for us. He calls above the tumult of the crowd of naysayers, above the brooding anxiety of a fallen world. In a thousand ways God calls us to believe. He calls when spring blossoms after the dead winter, when a baby is ushered into the world, when a friend touches you with kindness, when a prayer is whispered for your healing. All are the voice of the Father calling. Let's not turn away the divine Mercy waiting for us.

Another prayer that illustrates the fact that faith is often coupled with doubt is the prayer of the desperate father whose child's epilepsy had often "thrown him into fire or water" (9:22), imperiling his life. The father implored Jesus, 'If you can do anything, take pity on us and help us.'

"'If you can?' said Jesus. 'Everything is possible for him who believes.'

"Immediately the boy's father exclaimed, 'I do believe; help me overcome my unbelief!'" (Mark 9:24). And the boy was completely healed.

The father's experience is not unlike our own often-ambiguous faith. To "believe" in Greek means "to give one's heart to." The word "belief" has been impoverished and come to mean a head-over-heart intellectual assent, so that what we believe equates to what we think. For some, religious belief, then, implies a kind of suspension of the intellect.

But God, the Creator of the intellect, asks us to "give our hearts" as well as our heads to Him. We live in a fallen and shallow world blown by contrary winds, and we ourselves are bent away from this perfect One who asks for our hearts. Jesus was not offended by the father's ambiguity, but saw in his doubt the seed of faith, a sign that faith was alive and ready to grow. Jesus did not discount his small seed faith but called him to a stronger belief, even as He calls to us today.

Sometimes people think they don't belong in the church or that they shouldn't try to pray because their beliefs are not thoroughly set in stone. We all experience a God-given desire to know God, to be with Him, even when we find ourselves failing again and again to be like Him. He does not despair. Wherever you are on your journey through life, God planted a seed of faith in your heart the moment you were born. Even if you are plagued with doubts you can believe. God will help you because He has set His heart on you.

Who can explain how and why God chooses to touch a heart? Sometimes it is the most hardened of hearts, like the thief on the cross who had lived a life of disobedience and lawlessness. National networks televised the account of Brian Nichols, a murderer on his way to kidnap and murder a young woman, as he had done before. But he was stopped in his tracks by the word of the Lord.

That word came through the voice of a young woman who was herself stumbling back to God, and through the faithful voice of an author who wrote the words God told him to write without knowing what God had in mind for them. A simple passage from *The Purpose Driven Life* by Rick Warren captivated the heart of a hell-bound man and turned him around.

Who can explain it? Apart from the fierce love of God for the world and the incredible power of His Holy Spirit, there is no explanation. We need to let Him love us, to respond in simple faith, though riddled with doubt, and cling to the hope extended toward us. Saul of Tarsus. Nichols of Atlanta. There is nothing ambiguous about the love of God that pursues us wherever we are.

Chapter 9

A PRAYER OF AVAILABILITY

"Now the Lord came and stood and called as at other times,

'Samuel! Samuel!' And Samuel answered,

"Speak, for Your servant is listening" (1 Sam. 3:10).

Kathleen Norris, who returned to her childhood faith after many years of estrangement from God, finds that "prayer is not doing, but being. It is not words but the beyond words experience of coming into the presence of something much greater than oneself. It is an invitation to recognize holiness, and to utter simple words—'Holy, Holy, Holy'—in response."

Samuel received such an invitation to recognize holiness. He was only a child, perhaps 12 years of age when he became the assistant to the aged priest, Eli. His mother, Hannah, had kept her promise to give him to the Lord's service. God had answered her earnest prayers to end her barrenness and grant her a child.

When we read about Eli and his sons and all that went on in the child's environment, one wonders how Samuel became the great prophet he was. Scripture tells us that Eli was aware that his sons, Hophni and Phineas, had sex with women who came to the tabernacle doors. He knew that they took for themselves the best portions of the sacrificed meat, rather than those assigned them in the covenant. These were Samuel's "big brothers," and Eli, his mentor, who "honored his sons more than God" (1 Sam. 2:29), would be severely punished.

"Speak, Lord, for Your servant is listening." How is it that Samuel could speak such a prayer of openness and availability when he was surrounded by such role models? We must take into the equation the prayers of his mother. As she came to the place of worship for the yearly sacrifice, bringing her son a new hand-sewn robe, she must have anguished over the evil of Samuel's surroundings. But she had given him to God. God would overrule even the evil Samuel witnessed daily in the tabernacle. She would continue to pray as she had even before he was born.

Many of us have dedicated our own children under an Army flag or in a church sanctuary. God will honor that dedication. Don't despair if your child is distant from God now. Keep praying, keep believing. Remember what His Word says, "Train a child in the way he should go, and when he is old he will not turn from it" (Prov. 22:6). He may wander for a time, as many of us do, but he will return.

Recognition and Response

God used the counsel of weak Eli to help Samuel understand that the voice he heard was God's voice. Our Lord is not limited or frustrated by evil surroundings. He can make His voice heard, He can accomplish His will, even through people who are not living a life of obedience. When Samuel realized that God was speaking to him, he was ready to respond.

His obedience must have been costly. God would send severe judgment on Eli and on his house, and Samuel would bear the news to the old priest. God "would judge his family forever because of the sin he knew about; his sons made themselves contemptible, and he failed to restrain them ... the guilt of Eli's house will never be atoned for by sacrifice or offering" (1 Sam. 3:13-14).

Imagine these difficult words on the lips of a young boy who, from all we read, must have cared for old Eli. They worked side by side, and Samuel was quick to respond to Eli's call. Three times he got up in the night without complaint when he thought Eli was calling him. How would his message be received by the dissolute brothers and other members of the household? What made Samuel so ready, so quick to obey the voice of God?

Perhaps we think it's the kind of prayer only a child could make—a child who doesn't really know what the implications of such a prayer might be—how it could change his life. God doesn't call us to be careful, only to be obedient because we have given our hearts to him. Samuel prayed in the manner he did out of love. The God his mother had taught him to honor and pray to had spoken to him, had asked something of him. He would obey, regardless of the cost! Perhaps he did not even think much about what the cost would be.

It's a little like what happens in marriage. When a couple is in love, having chosen to be together forever, they do not think about what might happen down the road. They do not think that there might issue no children from this union, that financial reverses might plunge them into poverty, that one might contract a debilitating disease and possibly die. Perhaps they do think of possibilities, but if they do, their strong love for each other overrules potential troubles. With joyful anticipation they promise "For richer, for poorer, in sickness or in health."

This is the childlike faith God honors and wants His children to possess. Jesus said, "Unless you change and become like little children, you will never enter the kingdom of heaven" (Matt 18:3). We need not fear giving our hearts to God, for He plans only good for His children. We need not be anxious about the possible consequences of a prayer we make to God, because He has promised to be with us and bless us as we journey with Him.

Some years later, the prophet Isaiah would pray a similar prayer when he recognized an invitation to holiness. When he saw the Lord "high and lifted up" and heard the angels crying "Holy, holy, holy," he became instantly aware of his smallness and sinfulness. But God purged his iniquity and gave him a prophetic message of redemption. Isaiah was a grown man, but his childlike faith enabled him to respond, "Here I am, send me" (Isa. 6:8).

How will we respond when God calls for us?

Chapter 10

A PRAYER OF DEPENDENCE

"O our God ... we have no power to face this vast army
that is attacking us. We do not know what to do: but our
eyes are upon You" (2 Chron. 20:12).

This prayer by King Jehosaphat as he and his people faced enemies bent upon their destruction has much to teach us, who are often bewildered in the face of overwhelming evil in a world gone awry. God's people had come a long way from their declaration: "Some trust in chariots, and some in horses: but we trust in the name of the Lord our God" (Psalm 20:7). The people of Judah had turned away from the God who created, delivered, nourished, and sustained them, and found themselves confronted by the fierce Moabites and Ammonites who were poised for attack. God's people were besieged with fear.

So it was that Jehosaphat, king of Judah, "resolved to inquire of the Lord, and proclaimed a fast for all Judah" (2 Chron. 20:2). His lengthy prayer on behalf of his people begins at the point of recognition that God is almighty, the ruler over every nation, not just theirs, but of all nations everywhere. The people turned once again toward the Lord in worship and obedience. Affirming their complete trust in the God in whose "hand is power and might" and against whom "no one is able to stand," all Judah listened for the Lord in expectant hope. It wasn't only the men who prayed—those who would go into battle against their enemies—but their wives and children also waited on God.

How long they waited for God's answer, we don't know, but we read that God responded through the prophetic voice of Jahaziel, a Levite. "Do not be afraid or discouraged because of this vast army. For the battle is not yours, but God's" (1 Chron. 20:15). God had promised to fight for them as long as they trusted in Him and obeyed Him, but we know their pattern of disobedience and national and personal failure. It is our story as well.

We who have pledged our allegiance to God often find ourselves facing dreaded enemies that wage war against our souls. Fear, anger, bitterness, sorrow and death are enemies our Lord conquered long ago at the cross through His suffering and death. So long as we do battle against these things in our own strength, we are defeated, even as the men and women of Judah were defeated so many years ago. "Take up your positions" God said to His people, "stand firm and see the deliverance the Lord will give you .... Go out to face them tomorrow, and the Lord will be with you" (2 Chron 20:17).

When We Don't Know What to Do

What should we do when we don't know what to do? The wise writer of Proverbs, echoing Jehosaphat's prayer, gives guidance: "Trust in the Lord with all your heart, and lean not on your own understanding; in all your ways acknowledge Him, and He will make your paths straight" (3:5). The battle against evil is the Lord's battle—and He is for us. He will fight for us as He did for the children of Israel if we keep our eyes on Him. His Holy Spirit remains to stand with us and for us until the end when He will finally bring all things under His control.

Someone once asked Mrs. Albert Einstein if she understood the theory of relativity. "No," she responded, "but I know Albert, and he can be trusted." We may not understand all of God's laws, why they were written, and how they work for our good, but we can know God, and He can be trusted.

Expect An Answer

"For many people, prayer is either a pious ritual or a forlorn hope," writes William Barclay. "It should be a thing of burning expectation. Maybe our trouble is that what we want from God is our answer, and when we do not get it we do not recognize God's answer which always comes."

When God answers we can be sure that what He designs will be better than anything we might affect for ourselves. The story is told of the famed Scottish hero, Robert Bruce, who when fleeing his enemies took refuge in a cave and prayed for God's protection. While in the cave a spider wove a web across its entrance. His pursuers came to the cave, but seeing the spider web across its opening thought that if Bruce had entered, he would have broken the web. So they went on their way leaving Bruce still hidden in the cave. Later Bruce said, "Without God, a stone wall is as a spider web; with God a spider web is as a stone wall."

Jehosaphat appointed singers to move ahead of the army and sing praises to God. With expectant joy they sang, "Praise the Lord, For His mercy endures forever." With minds focused on God rather than on their difficulties, their whole outlook changed from despair to hope, and God rewarded their trust. We read that "As they began to sing and praise Him (for the splendor of His holiness), the Lord set ambushes against the men of Ammon, Moab and Mount Seir, who were invading Judah, and they were defeated" (2 Chron. 20:22).

Over and over throughout Scripture comes the instruction to praise and thank God in everything—the difficult and the easy. We are most happy and at peace when we are aware of the goodness of God and when in humble, thankful spirit, we acknowledge all He has given, all that He is. How it breaks the chains of sadness and bitterness! "The chains that seem to bind you fall powerless behind you when you praise the Lord." The modern lyric echoes what we know about the wonder-working power of thankfulness, which keeps us focused on Him who is all Love. In *The Imitation of Christ*, Thomas a' Kempis wrote: "He who loves God with all his heart dreads neither death, torment, judgment nor hell, for perfect love opens a sure passage to God."

Even in the face of perplexing evil and death, we can pray the prayer of utter dependence: "O our God ... we don't know what to do, but our eyes are upon You."

Moving Inward Through Prayer

Author Walker Percy asks, "Why is it possible to learn more in ten minutes about the Crab Nebula in kTaurus, which is 6,000 light-years away, than you presently know about yourself, even though you've been stuck with yourself all your life?" St. Augustine knew where to go to learn about himself. "Oh God, I pray You to let me know my self." The Psalmist wrote: "He leads me beside the still waters, He restores my soul" (Psalm 23:2-3). Prayer connects us not only to God but to our true selves.

As God draws us closer to the divine center, we begin to see ourselves as God sees us and to unwrap the layers of pretense, prejudice and pride that we are prone to in this fallen world.

The Apostle Paul expressed his yearning "to know Christ and the power of His resurrection and the fellowship of sharing in His sufferings, becoming like Him in his death, and so, somehow, to if attain to the resurrection from the dead" (Phil. 3:10-11). This is the prayer of all who would experience His presence in their lives.

The journey inward to discover our true selves often involves suffering. Like waves breaking against the rocks, the troubles of life threaten to wear away our courage and weaken our resolve, but Christ is our strength. Jesus "learned patience through the things He suffered" (Heb. 5:8), and we too are called to bear our burdens patiently. In the midst of turmoil, He leads us beside the quiet waters of His presence where we are able to embrace our true selves and reflect His enduring image.

Chapter 11

THE PRAYER OF TRANSPARENCY

"Search me, O God, and know my heart; test me and know my anxious thoughts. See if there is any offensive way in me, and lead me in the way everlasting" (Psalm 139:23-24).

Few of us are willing to be totally transparent, to be searched and tested and scrutinized. We are justifiably grateful that our thoughts are private, our anxieties at least controllable on the outside. We are careful to keep the vulnerable self protected from onlookers, from acquaintances, from those we spend time with socially. Even in our most intimate relationships—a spouse or lifetime friend—we often feel we cannot let our innermost selves be seen. After all, what might happen if they always knew just what we were thinking or feeling? Whom can we trust with such vital information?

People suffering from paranoid schizophrenia fear that others can hear their thoughts and read their minds. Some hear voices addressing their most intimate thoughts and secrets. Others believe that unseen forces are directing them to act in specific ways.

Healthy persons know their thoughts are private, that the innermost self is "the one insular Tahiti," as author Herman Melville put it. We guard this anonymity carefully, hugging ourselves to ourselves , trusting only ourselves. Yet, for all our fear of total intimacy, we still yearn for it. Strange, this hide and seek game of the heart. We hide but continue to call out clues to our whereabouts.

This desire to be known and understood at the deepest level of ourselves moves us toward filial forms—emotional and sexual—and if we're lucky we find intimacy in marriage, the union that most approaches the divine unity. Marriage satisfies on one level, but there remains a place unfilled in even the most ideal human relationship. We are aware of a hunger unassuaged, a piece of ourselves without a home. We often live for years with the gnawing sense that no one truly knows the real person we are, that we can never trust anyone to understand us.

There is one all-seeing eye, One before whom all is known and nothing is hidden. He is God, who designed us for intimate relationship with Himself. The prophet Zechariah writes of "the eyes of the Lord, which range throughout the earth" (4:10). The Prophet Samuel knew that "man looks on the outward appearance, but God looks on the heart" (1 Sam. 16:7). In the New Testament, the Apostle Paul reminds us that "He will bring to light what is hidden in darkness and will expose the motives of men's hearts" (1 Cor. 4:5).

God created us to experience with Him an intimacy unlike any other. It is both the culmination of our whole purpose and the foundation of meaningful relationships in the world. The theologian speaks of the "God-shaped vacuum" in us all that can only be filled with the One for whom our souls long. "Oh, that I knew where to find Him," Job lamented (23.3). Why does it seem He hides from us if indeed He yearns for us as He says?

"Behold I ... knock," Jesus says. "If you will open the door, I'll come in and sup with you and you with Me (see Rev. 3:20 NKJV). The image of the Savior standing outside our heart's door is poignant and riveting. So is that little tender word "sup" that sounds like "suck," as in a baby taking nourishment from its mother.

Many are the assurances that God desires us with a love that is jealous as a lover's, fierce as any protector's and enduring as a mother's. Such a grand truth is difficult to explain in human terms. "I have loved you with an everlasting love," God says in Jer. 31:3. And Jesus weeping over Jerusalem said, "How often I have longed to gather your children together as a hen gathers her chicks under her swings, but you were not willing" (Matt. 23:37). The depth of His desire to draw us to Himself is never more clearly underscored than in the image of the suffering Savior bleeding for the souls of His loved ones.

The Joy of Knowing God

Sometimes it seems that God hides from us in thick darkness. Or is the gloom our own hesitance to open up to Him in complete disclosure of our naked selves? Are we willing to say to Him, "Search me, O God, and see my thoughts?" Or do we pretend that we are not lost souls who have strayed from our purpose to love God with all our hearts and to love our neighbor as ourselves? Do we hide from Him, pretend that we are not "wretched, pitiful, poor, blind and naked," without the covering of our Savior's blood (see Rev. 3:17)?

When we come to God, it must be in complete humility and repentance. When Isaiah "saw the Lord high and lifted up," he immediately became aware of his own sinfulness and repented. Humility is the first qualification for intimacy with Him.

Jesus said "whoever has My commands and obeys them, he is the one who loves Me. He who loves Me, will be loved by my Father, and I too will love him and show Myself to him." (John 14:21). Daily obedience to God makes it possible for us to have the kind of intimacy that infuses our lives with meaningful, even glorious possibility and power.

St. Paul's perennial prayer was that he would "know Him (Jesus) and the power of His resurrection and the fellowship of sharing in His sufferings, becoming like Him in His death" (Phil. 3:10). Obedience may call us to suffering, for suffering is the way of the cross. Christians pledge to "take up the cross daily and follow Him." The price may be high, but the rewards of a life lived in complete unison with God's will and design are unparalleled.

"What things were gain to me ... I count as rubbish," said Paul, compared to knowing Christ. In writing to the Ephesians, Paul lists the spiritual blessings that are ours through knowing Him: "He chose us ... adopted us as His sons ... redeemed us ... has forgiven our sins, and made known to us the mystery of His will" (1:4-9).

He is the ultimate significance in life, the reason for it, the beginning of it, and the end of it. Intimacy with our Creator is the greatest joy we can experience. All satisfaction, happiness, peace and virtue are wrapped up in Him who has embraced us with His life and calls us to walk daily hand in hand with Him.

Chapter 12

A PRAYER OF INTEGRITY

"May the words of my mouth and the meditation of my heart be pleasing in Your sight, O Lord, my Rock and my Redeemer" (Psalm 19:14).

When I was growing up in The Salvation Army, this prayer was used as a benediction at every meeting of the YPL (Young People's Legion). The prayer would seal what had hopefully been our motive for fellowship in the first place. That we sometimes repeated the words of the prayer thoughtlessly in our hurry to get on to the next exciting event is doubtless true, but nonetheless, the very practice of that prayer made indelible impressions on our minds that lingered after decades of living. And what could be more appropriate for young or old than underscoring this timeless and unremitting bond between word and deed?

Like love and marriage or a horse and carriage, word and deed go together. Words contrary to actions can weaken deeds, and deeds in conflict with what we say can nullify the words we use. They are inexplicably tied together, bringing integrity to our lives. "Do not merely listen to the word. ... Do what it says," wrote the Apostle James (1:22). It is possible to say with our mouth that we belong to Christ and by our actions deny that claim. As Richard Foster puts it, "We cannot <u>preach</u> good news and <u>be</u> bad news."

Jesus told the story of two sons who were asked by their father to go into the field and perform a required task. One said he would not go, but changed his mind and went. The other son quickly agreed to go, but did not carry out his promise. Jesus asked his listeners which one really did the will of the father. Words were not enough; action was required. Words only make sound sense when backed up by suitable deeds.

Wisdom Makes Uncommon Sense

The Greeks believed that if a person had both wisdom and common sense, he would be perfectly equipped for life. Paul taught that Jesus brings us knowledge of eternal things—the spiritual knowledge that satisfies our questions about life here and hereafter. He also exemplifies the common sense power to solve the practical problems of every day living. These were hallmarks of His teaching.

Where did He get this wisdom? The people raised in Jesus' home district pondered that question. They could not believe this Man of Galilee was the fulfillment of Isaiah's prophecy that the Messiah would be "a rod from the stem of Jesse ... a Branch that would grow out of his roots. The Spirit of the Lord (would) rest upon Him, the Spirit of wisdom and understanding, the Spirit of counsel and might, the Spirit of knowledge and of the fear of the Lord" (Isaiah 11:1-2).

It's not surprising that people sought Jesus' opinion on current events like the fall of a tower, the threats of Herod, the violence of Pilate, the moral puzzle of a man being born blind, rival miracle workers, etc. It's significant to note how often Jesus refused to speculate, to argue merely theoretical questions, or to "explain" theological puzzles. Sometimes He turned questions around to bring conviction to the heart: "You repent, never mind other people's sins!" And if occasionally he was warned of danger to Himself, He merely affirmed the divine plan for His career and continued His mission with calm courage.

His impartiality, insight, and good sense made His counsel valuable even on nonreligious topics. The New Testament relates the occasion when Jesus observed guests maneuvering for seats at the head table and remarked that it is wiser to take lower seats and be invited higher than to take higher seats and be told to move down. He advised litigants to compromise before going to court—it's cheaper. He quoted the familiar proverb about pearls thrown to swine, to urge discrimination before entering into religious arguments with people desiring only to debate.

He gave some perceptive advice, showing that in an occupied country it's better when commandeered to walk a mile carrying military baggage, to offer to go further voluntarily than to resent every step with bitterness of soul. Equally shrewd is His counsel that worry is a wasted exercise since it can't add to one's height or change the color of the hair (see Matthew 5:41, 6:25-34).

Jesus Our Source of Wisdom

Integrity in both word and deed made Jesus a wise counselor. His wisdom was unimpeachable, His power invincible, His love complete. And we who have been adopted into His family have been given the inheritance of wisdom and sound sense that is so desperately needed in these days. The Holy Spirit who teaches us points us to Jesus who says "Take My yoke upon you and learn from Me" (Matthew 11:29).

It is through the covenant and action of prayer that we learn the wisdom of Jesus. The exercise involves more than rhetoric or the repetition of pious phrases. Jesus urged His followers not to "keep on babbling like pagans, for they think they will be heard because of their many words" (Matthew 6:7). In giving Christians a model prayer, Jesus coupled words with the positive actions of forgiving, fasting and believing. The words we use are important, but far more valuable is the genuine attitude of heart that enters into the praise and petition of prayer with the whole heart and waits for God's wise guidance.

"Who is wise and understanding among you?" James asks. "Let him show it by his good life, by deeds done in the humility that comes from wisdom" (James 3:13). Words of the mouth and meditation of the heart—an unbeatable combination that God will accept and honor. This is a legacy we can claim through regular fellowship with the Source of all wisdom. How He loves to lavish His resources on us.

Richard Foster writes, "The love of the Father is like a sudden rain shower that will pour forth when you least expect it, catching you up into wonder and praise. ... When this happens, do not put up an umbrella to protect yourself but rather stand in the drenching rain of the Father."

Chapter 13

A Prayer of Disappointment

"My God, My God, why have You forsaken Me?"

(Matt. 27:46, Psalm 22:1)

Jesus prayed this prayer from the cross as He hung dying for the sin of all mankind. His experience remains unique, never to be repeated in the history of the world, but we who are followers of this sinless, triumphant Christ will have moments in our lives when we feel that God has hidden Himself from us, that He has absconded and left us in terrible distress.

Jesus' cry of abandonment was uttered by David centuries earlier and recorded in the 22nd Psalm. "Why are You so far from helping me, and from the words of my groaning?" Who has not experienced those times when Heaven seems shut up against us, when, as George Buttrick writes, "we beat on Heaven's door with bruised knuckles in the dark"?

Why? It's the desperate cry of human experience through the ages. Consider Abraham whom God promised would become the father of a great nation. Two decades passed before he and Sarah received the first hint—one small boy—that God was doing anything about that promise. Think of Joseph left by so-called loved ones to die in a pit. Time crawled slowly by as he heard no word from God about this terrible injustice. Elijah endured the wind, the earthquake and the fire as he waited in anguish for the still small voice of God. Why?

What Can We Expect From God?

Atheists cannot feel disappointed in God. They expect nothing. They receive nothing. But we who give our lives to God have a right to expect something in return, don't we? So what does it mean when the God who said "I will be with you always" doesn't seem to be there when we most desperately need Him?

Why Isn't He More Direct With Us?

In Old Testament times, God communicated directly with His people, leaving no room for doubt. He wanted them to believe Him, to rely upon Him. But God's directness seemed to produce the opposite effect of lasting faith. His people responded with fear and open rebellion.

The life of faith is a growing relationship with the God who longs to love and be loved. It is a sojourn meant to develop in mutual freedom. He grants us the freedom to respond to Him, and we must grant Him that same freedom. Perhaps the times when we feel forsaken involves the development of this loving relationship, which is what prayer is all about.

How could we love a God whom we could command? God is no genie in a bottle. He is the great I AM who is Mystery and Majesty. If we could command Him to come at our beck and call, we would not be in relationship to the great God of the universe who is greater than anyone or even any idea of greatness.

We think how wonderful it would be to actually hear His voice, to have no doubt whatever about His will in every situation. The Israelites enjoyed such a direct relationship with God, but God was too holy, too great for intimacy. He was so holy that they could not even come near the Most Holy Place for fear of being killed. They lamented, "Let us not ... see this great fire anymore, or we will die" (Deuteronomy 18:16). We cannot endure the full force of unfiltered sunlight. Isaiah asked, "Who of us can dwell with the consuming Fire "that is Almighty God? (33:14 NKJV).

God's reason for creating the human community was to have fellowship with us, to love and be loved forever. To accomplish that, a new covenant was needed, one based on forgiveness and grace. The new covenant would further remind us that life is more than the few years we spend on this planet, that ultimately Christ's sacrifice on the Cross would annihilate every evil deed, every weakness, every tear. "Because He lives, we too shall live." Our fallen world includes suffering and pain while we await the full coming of Christ's kingdom. That world can be called the valley in which His kingdom is growing within us.

Soul Making in the Valley

St. John of the Cross spoke of the "Dark Night of the Soul" as an experience that teaches us faith in God alone. When suddenly everything seems dark and the light has gone out of life, we begin to question ourselves, our motivations. We examine ourselves to see if our acts are inspired by pride or faith, selfishness or love.

The dark night of the soul has been described in Scripture as a desert—dry, barren, lonely. When we feel completely alone and unable to discern the presence of the God who promised to be with us, we need to remember that felt absence is not literal absence. If God is love as Scripture says, there must be a reason for His silences. What are we to understand by His behavior?

When we feel forsaken, that is the time to wait on God, to trust in the character of God who does not lie. He is working out all things for your good, and He is as good as His word. Don't give up your most precious faith or allow your dryness to lead you to despair. When every loved one has left you and every material possession is lost, faith endures—not just for this life, but for the next.

Allow your dryness of soul to lead you to prayer. With all distractions gone, even all warm fellowship, you can focus on God alone. I often think about Mary who waited in the garden after everyone had fled in despair. She trusted in the profound and infinite mercy of the Lord she had come to know, and she waited where she had last experienced the reality of Christ's presence. Jesus knows the loneliness of the desert and the desolation of the cross. His victory is our victory if we stay in the garden a little longer and wait for Him and for His perfect plan to be revealed.

Come to the Waters...

(Isaiah 55:1)

POEMS OF INSPIRATION

A Prayer in Wait

The army on the facing hill
waits in ambush, sharpens its sword
and, finding its moment, spills
into our peace. The frightening horde
advances, blood in their cold eyes,
but faith is in our own and flies
upward in quick and sure appeal.
We have known God's power to heal
in days gone by. And shall we now
faint before this present foe?
O, Lord, show us how
to let our quaking fears go
and when we don't know what to do
keep our eyes intent on You.

PROMISE

"Our God shall come and shall not be silent" (Psalm 50:3).

He comes ... in the thundering tumble of wind
Down a greening hill
When all the world is wrapped in Him.
He comes in a ballerina dance
Of chartreuse and rosy silk—
Virginal maid of beauty
Lingering on the mind, promising
Something you cannot forget.
He comes to the wintering ground—
Ravished, silent, spent—
And wakens it to joy.
In everything He whispers, thunders,
Comforts, weeps, and laughs.
"Our God shall come and shall not be silent."

MUSINGS IN AN UPPER ROOM

Lord, how You frighten us,
coming through walls, suddenly appearing,
all shining, unearthly. Can it be
You're the smiling One we remember
bouncing children on your knee?

We remember Your hillside stories,
so terrible and wonderful,
but all their awe inspiring glories,
their woundings and their soothings were
gentled by some calm or ease
we felt with You. We marked the real
way Your lips formed words and sighs,
the way dust clung to Your heel
when You walked the village roads, the arch
of muscle and bone when You stooped to kneel.

And when You died, Your blood was red.
It matted Your hair, fell on your chest.
We could see it pound, and we fled
when we recognized Your innocence,
that you were dying for us instead.
They put You in a human tomb.
Women wept, as women do,
as many touched with grief and gloom.
(Once, Lord, we saw You weep
tears like rain in the silent room.)

Resurrected, now You stand
too wonderful for us to look,
too high, we cannot comprehend
Your majesty, Your holiness.
But suddenly You extend a hand.
What are these marks we see?
The wounds, the ragged gashes?
Marks of experienced humanity!
Why have you allowed these to remain
in Your splendid, glorified body?

Reminders always of mankind's son?
Marks of earth You choose to wear?
Can it be when all is said and done
these bloody badges forever prove
that You and I are inexplicably one?

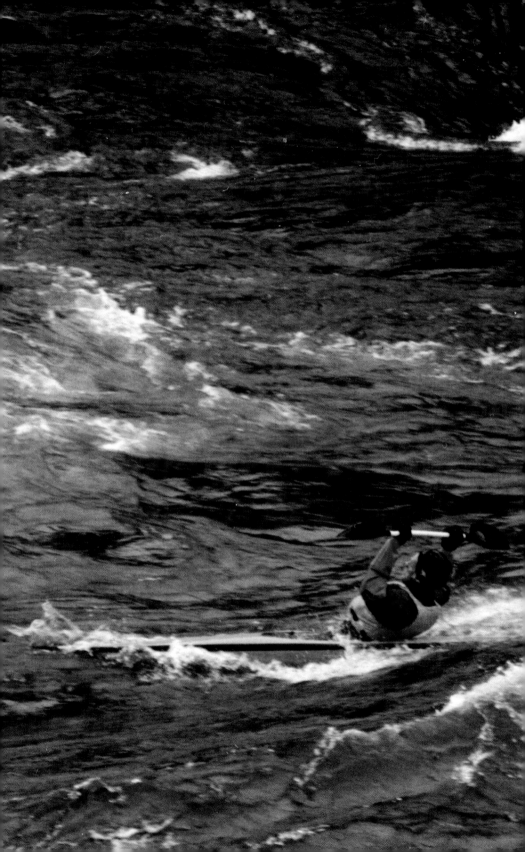

A Prayer in Peril

Winds of war blow a maelstrom,
clouds of terror threaten.
Trembling in the pending hailstorm
the waves of panic set in.

Our little craft is tossed and blown,
no match for a raging sea
You seem to sleep, unaware, unknown
in the hour of tragedy.

Wake us from this fitful slumber,
our little faith increase.
Open our eyes to see with wonder
Christ – our hope and peace

The Source

We think we pull from within—
our resources, our fortitude—
but it is God,
His wisdom in our absurdity,
His love in our studied neglect.

We reach for the hem of His robe,
dimly aware of Him,
but even unknowing, it is God;
it is always God
who in our frail spirits prevails.

THREE-FOLD PRAISE TO CHRIST OUR LORD

Christ is the image of the invisible God, the firstborn over all creation. For by Him all things were created, things in heaven and on earth, visible and invisible, whether thrones or powers or rulers or authorities; all things were created by Him and for Him. He is before all things, and in Him all things hold together. And He is the head of the body, the church; He is the beginning and the firstborn from among the dead, so that in everything He might have the supremacy. For God was pleased to have all His fullness dwell in Him, and through Him to reconcile to Himself all things, whether things on earth or things in heaven, by making peace through His blood, shed on the cross (Col. 1:15-20).

The Cosmic Christ
Poised above the constellations,
planets pirouette at His feet and
stars stream from His fingertips.
From His lips the four winds swirl
across the heavens, down mountain peaks,
churning ocean waves that roll and roar
and crash to the music of His great soul.
Green plains, swollen with praise,
burst with goldenrod, purple heather,
jack pine and lily, rhododendron and rose.
Watching with eyes that never sleep,
He cradles His universe child.
Yet some deep yearning
stirs His heart, and man emerges,
released from a resplendent Womb.
A living soul to share His heart!
A mind to know His thoughts!
Heaven erupts in spontaneous joy
to lullaby the children of His love.

The Incarnate Christ
The angels bow in ignorant remorse,
their praise mellowed by His pain
as His love children traverse the earth

without an upward glance,
intent on their small subduing
of a world they claim as theirs.
Love compels Him from His throne.
The Creator becomes the created.
Mewling, cooing, flailing infant arms
in which galaxies once danced,
the Holy Babe is suckled at human breasts.
Hands that fashioned stars
now hammer rude planks.
He walks among them, the God-man,
knowing intimately human need,
healing the deaf, the blind, the dead.
Soon enough, holy hands and feet
learn the hammer's rage.
The tree Omnipotence planted holds Him
suspended between earth and heaven

The Triumphant King

Down the years His blood has flowed,
a river, wide enough, deep enough
to consume the wild rages of sin.
Beneath its pure waves men have plunged
to find themselves alive as He.
Alive to love that shimmers, dances
and compels their homeward hearts.
Once more He leaves the hearth of heaven
to guide His children home.
This time, no mewling, cooing Babe
but the King emblazoned with glory
and dazzling in holy light.
See Him recall the four winds,
coil the oceans in His robe,
wrap up stars and galaxies in His train.
Fashioned in purity and shining joy,
His Bride rises to meet her Lord!

BREATHING LESSONS

I need some breathing lessons.
Inhale, exhale, inhale
all that's fresh and pure
and just the right amount.
Or is there no limit
to the capacity of these lungs?
Exhale, inhale, exhale
all that is useless, spent.
Is it automatic?
No, I'm breathless—straining, gasping.
My rhythm's off;
I'm dying by degrees.
Spirit, rescue me and teach me how
to live. Give me
Soul to soul
resuscitation.

A Prayer At Times

I have respect for Your timing, Lord–
in retrospect.
But at the moment of my yearning,
when need is burning in my bones,
my spirit groans
with urgent pleas and rigid rationale.
Passion all but consumes me
in a blazing ball of want.

Help me, Lord, to remember this,
not only in the bliss
of memory but now that Your grace,
perfect like Your timing,
transcends all time and space.

"I wait for the Lord, my soul waits, and in His word I put my hope"
(Psalm 130:5).

Fragility

I try to keep my prayers in order:
Worship first, then praise
for Your manifold grace.
but the list is so long, and I—
I am a dry sapling in the sun
gasping with need
down to my scorched roots.
I'm wilting, fainting, famished.
Please—a drink from your rich store
and I shall not ask for more ...
until next I need You like this.

Confession

O Eternal Fount,
I've been sipping Your life
through a straw
when poised like a mighty flood
You've been waiting
to pour Yourself
over me!

Supply And Demand

How crude your manger, Lord,
A feeding trough
from which the beasts ate
until it was empty, dry.

Your swaddled body, pure
hallowed it.
Uncommon light and grace
filled every part.

I feel my heart a manger,
a feeding trough
from which the world eats
until I am empty, dry.

But if the Christ shall lie
holy pure,
inside its common shell,
filling every part,

the world of men may take
and not deplete
that ever-fresh supply
of Living Bread.

Good Friday Prayer

You wept over Jerusalem
and sweat great drops of blood.
We scarcely notice other souls
until they interrupt our lives.
The Father's will was Your meat,
Your drink, Your vital breath.
but we, Your selfish children, do only
what seems good to us,
and when you don't play by our rules,
we take our hearts like hoarded playthings
and stumble wounded home.

Teach us how to weep again
out of righteous hearts that hate
the dark savagery of men.
Keep the pain of others in our eyes
like stains of indelible ink
mirroring our dead soul's blight
that only blood can wash away.
Keep us in the place, O Lord,
where those sweaty drops can fall on us.
Humble our passionate hearts until
they beat as one with Yours.

ARPEGGIO

We're no prodigies, Lord,
but novices—
unpracticed children
pledged to the Master.
We struggle with prayer's rhythm,
its mystic melodies
and artful harmonies.
Please keep marking time
in our prayer-tuned ears
until our noise is music
to delight Your heart.

THE UNCONTAINABLE

The Uncontainable
bridges the vaulted dome of sky,
rides the wind from east to west,
and cups oceans in His Hands.
Who can hold him—
Master of the Universe, Holy One—
Who fills every space?

Chapter 14

THE PRAYER OF SUFFERING FAITH

"Though He slay me, yet will I trust Him" (Job 13:15, KJV).

How could Job say these words? What would bring him to such a conclusion about God after all he had suffered—loss of family, friends, home, possessions, sight, and health? Did he really mean it? Perhaps he was mad or deluded.

A parody of the old adage says, "If you can keep your head when all around are losing theirs, you probably don't understand the situation."

I think I could understand Job's statement if it had been made after God confronted him in person and finally spoke to him. He would likely have been so astonished by this visitation that he might have forgotten everything else. Eloquently God "explained Himself" (though He never cited His reasons for allowing Job to suffer as he did).

He urged Job to consider all the evidence of His greatness and wisdom visible in creation—from the habits of small defenseless birds to the great leviathan; from cosmic storms to quiet eddying streams. The "appearance" of the great God of the universe was unbelievably frightening and humbling, for Job repented in sackcloth and ashes, admitting that he had spoken of things he knew nothing about.

We might understand Job's statement of implicit trust in the Lord despite everything if it had come after he heard from God Himself. "Truly, I uttered what I did not understand—things too wonderful for me that I did not know ... my eye sees You. Therefore I abhor myself, and repent in dust and ashes" (Job 42:6). But Job's declaration that he would trust God even if he were killed came before the Lord appeared to him. He had nothing left but the dubious comfort of a few friends. Even his wife had given up trying to understand her husband and urged him to "curse God and die." Her reaction is completely understandable. We might have given the same advice if we had witnessed such dire treatment of a loved one.

How was Job to interpret the devastating turn his life had taken? He had been an upright person. He held fast to his innocence in spite of incredible pressure to sway him from such a boast. If he had committed some sin, he would have understood and probably been willing to take his punishment like a man. But he knew he didn't deserve what was happening to him.

Moreover, everyone in his neighborhood knew that suffering came as a result of sin. It was an undisputed, though erroneous, fact. Therefore, Job was a sinner. It was as simple as that. Why couldn't he accept it like everyone else?

Getting Inside the Miracle

It is natural to want to understand why something happens to us. We want to know how things work, why we respond as we do. We want to wrap our minds around the great mysteries and solve them. Can it be that there are some mysteries too great for us to unravel? It has long been our downfall that we attempt to "understand" God with our minds. G. K. Chesterton writes, "It is only the fool who tries to get the heavens inside his head and not unnaturally his head bursts. The wise man is content to get his head inside the heavens."

Only a profound faith in God could have made Job repudiate the prevailing "truths" about himself and about his suffering. Only faith could have brought him to march to the beat of a different drummer—the heartbeat of a God who could not be so neatly pinned down or put into the construct of man's small mind.

"God is a self–concealer as well (as self–revealer)," writes Philip Yancey. "The secret things belong to the Lord our God, Moses told the Israelites, but the things revealed belong to us and to our children forever. We live dangling between the secret things, withheld perhaps for our own protection, and the revealed things. The God who satisfies our thirst is also the great Unknown—the one no one can look upon and live. Perhaps it takes God's absence and presence both for us to remain ourselves, or even to survive."

We embrace God by faith in His inscrutable and unfailing love. "Without faith, it is impossible to please [Him]," writes the author of Hebrews (11:6). We do not please Him by pursuing Him with our intellect alone as we work out the gift of faith in our lives. We must begin by recognizing our utter helplessness to save ourselves and to live the life God created us for. We must cast ourselves upon His grace. The gospel at its profoundest point stands in utter contradiction to human wisdom, writes Gordon Fee. "God has redeemed our fallen race by means of the ultimate contradiction in terms, a crucified Messiah."

By faith in that crucified Messiah we approach God and only that way. "Neither is there salvation in any other; for there is none other name under heaven given among men, whereby we must be saved" (Acts 4:12). Further, we read that one day "every knee will bow" at the name of Jesus Christ (Rom. 14:11).

How does one get Job's kind of faith—a faith in utter contradiction to human wisdom? From God who is our source for everything. He gives to "everyone a measure of faith" and promises to increase our faith as we exercise the gift He has given. When it is hard, when no one else believes, when it makes no sense by human standards, we keep on trusting. This kind of believing faith—faith that perseveres in the face of suffering—may only be a tiny seed at the beginning, but as we live in its nourishing environment, faith grows until one day we can say, even as Job did, "Though He slay me, I'll still trust Him."

Chapter 15

A Prayer of Deliverance

"The Assyrian kings have laid waste these nations and their lands. They have thrown their gods into the fire and destroyed them, for they were not gods but only wood and stone, fashioned by men's hands. Now, O Lord our God, deliver us from his hand, so that all kingdoms on earth may know that You alone, O Lord, are God" (2 Kings 19:17–20).

Judah was about to embark on one of its most formidable challenges. Faced with terror and death at the hand of Assyria, they were in danger of complete annihilation—except for one thing. Their God, maker of heaven and earth, had given them a promise. Hezekiah would hold the Lord to that promise with all the faith he possessed.

The small remnant located in Judah where, according to archaeological evidence, many Israelites had fled during the Assyrian assaults, also was weak militarily, with the Judahite army consisting largely of foot soldiers. The mighty Assyrians possessed a strong military of able horsemen and fast chariots.

Their king, Sennacherib, taunted Judah's King Hezekiah: "On what are you basing this confidence of yours?" (2 Kings 18:19). He urged the people not to listen to Hezekiah who believed the Lord would deliver them. Pointing to his other conquests, Sennacherib jeers, "How ... can the Lord deliver Jerusalem from my hand?" (2 Kings 18:35).

In an earlier coup, God had allowed the country to be overtaken as a judgment due to disobedience. Sennacherib claimed to have captured 46 of Hezekiah's fortified cities and taken the people captive, enforcing heavy tribute in gold and silver. Now he threatened to take Jerusalem, demanding Judah's complete surrender on the very spot where the prophet Isaiah had earlier warned King Ahaz (Hezekiah's predecessor) to trust in God rather than make an alliance with Assyria.

A Time for Tears

When King Hezekiah heard the threat of the Assyrian tyrant that his country would be utterly destroyed, he tore his clothes and put on sackcloth to express his anguish and outrage against the Assyrian blasphemy of their God. Indeed it was a time for tears. Their way of life, including their religious freedom, was threatened by an imposing giant that had successfully worn down such nations as Sepharvaim, Hena, Ivahy and Samaria. How could little Judah defend itself against such an enemy?

Assyria also attempted to drive a wedge between Judah's King Hezekiah and the people by exploiting any resentment that might have existed among those who opposed his reforms. We read in verse 4 of 2 Kings 18 that Hezekiah "removed the high places, smashed the sacred stones and cut down the Asherah poles" (symbols of idolatry) and returned to a worship of the living God. Not everyone thought that was a good idea and they criticized their sovereign for his political incorrectness.

Is it too great a stretch to compare this 7th century predicament with our own in the 21st? Terrorist groups bent on our annihilation taunt America, belittle our traditions—especially our God. They employ sophisticated weapons and operate through a wide, political network in their efforts to make even the greatest country in the free world tremble.

We express our distress as we nightly view the deaths of brave men and women fighting for our freedom. The sackcloth we wear is coarse and grating against the fabric of souls accustomed to liberty. Our leader is criticized and bears the weight of difficult decisions. We need to pray for him and encourage him to respond as Hezekiah did.

A Time For Remembrance

The prophet Isaiah encouraged Judah not "to be afraid of what you have heard—those words with which the underlings of the king of Assyria have blasphemed (God)." He assured them that God was stronger than any Assyrian army and that Sennacherib would be "cut down with the sword" (2 Kings 19:4-7).

Hezekiah had inherited the bad decisions of a former regime. Often we reap the results of a bad past decision—our own or someone else's—but God is greater than even our worst decision and deadliest detour away from Him. Isaiah had "read the back of the book" and knew what the ending would be. We who belong to Christ are likewise assured of victory. However bleak the tragedies of this life, however fierce the enemy of our souls appears, we will overcome them in Christ who sealed our victory at the cross. We have won—even before the battle begins!

A Time for Prayer

"Surely you have heard what the kings of Assyria have done to all the countries, destroying them completely," Sennacherib jeered. "And will you be delivered?" (2 Kings 19:11). Spreading this message out before the Lord in the Temple, Hezekiah prayed: "O Lord, God of Israel ... You alone are God over all the Kingdoms of the earth ... listen to the words Sennacherib has sent to insult the living God" (2 Kings 19:15-16).

Hezekiah acknowledged that God was greater than all, and he prayed for deliverance "so that all kingdoms of earth may know that You alone, O Lord, are God" (2 Kings 19:19).

And God responded! "I will defend this city and save it for my sake and for the sake of David my servant" (2 Kings 19:34). The chronicler tells us, "the angel of the Lord ... put to death 185,000 men in the Assyrian camp" (2 Kings 19:35).

When our hearts are right before God, He delivers us from the destroyer and preserves our souls, which are precious to Him. Our enemy is more formidable than Sennacherib and his threats have eternal significance, but he is no match for the King of kings. Do you stand thoroughly in His camp? If so, you can wait and see the deliverance of God. "The Lord will watch over your coming and going both now and forevermore" (Psalm 121:8).

Chapter 16

THE PRAYER OF PERSISTENCE

"[We] should always pray and not give up" (Luke 18:1).

Psalm 22 is a pulsating study in contrasts. In one breath the author complains that God seems to have forsaken him, and in the next he affirms his trust in God and offers consistent praise.

"Why are you so far from saving me, so far from the words of my groaning?" he asks. "O my God, I cry out by day, but You do not answer, by night, and am not silent" (1–2). "But You, O Lord, be not far off; O my Strength, come quickly to help me" (19). David makes a similar complaint in the first two verses of Psalm 13: "How long, O Lord? Will you forget me forever? How long will You hide Your face from me? How long must I wrestle with my thoughts and every day have sorrows in my heart? How long will my enemy triumph over me?"

Is the writer about to give up and turn his back on God who has promised to hear and answer quickly? No, hear his quick affirmation: "But I trust in Your unfailing love; my heart rejoices in Your salvation. I will sing to the Lord, for He has been good to me" (13:1-6). What do we make of these conflicting expressions?

How do we put the Lord's delays in the context of His promise that "before they call, I will answer; while they are yet speaking I will hear" (Isa. 65:24)? Clearly, Jesus taught that "we should always pray and not give up" (Luke 18:1). The implication is that we who call upon Him could get weary as we wait, even grow "faint" before we are sure that God is hearing and answering.

God's promise to hear and answer promptly is not really a contradiction of our experience. Though we sometimes wait many years before a prayer is answered, we can be sure God will respond because He has promised to do so. When we begin to feel our faith slipping it's important to remember that the whole idea behind prayer is relationship. Through spending time with God, we are learning about Him and His desires for us. A prayer may very well change as we begin to understand more and more who God is.

But often a prayer that we are sure is in keeping with the will and purposes of God sometimes seems to fall on deaf ears. A prayer for a loved one to turn in faith to God, for instance, is certainly in accordance with our Lord's love and mercy. It is His desire that all men know Him. "He is patient with you, not wanting anyone to perish, but everyone to come to repentance" (2 Pet. 3:9). And since Jesus has said, "If we ask anything according to His will, He hears us" (1 John 5:14), we can expect for that loved one to be saved, can't we?

From the time I was a small child I prayed for the salvation of my father who was famous for saying, "All that religious nonsense is just a lot of hooey. There's nothing beyond; when you're dead, that's all there is." My childhood came and went and my prayers, in varying degrees of intensity, continued for his salvation, but he remained entrenched in his agnosticism. I had to accept that though God longed for his salvation, He had to be invited into my father's life. It wasn't until he lay dying that we discovered Dad had been reading the Bible I'd given him for his birthday.

Jesus tells a story to show the importance of continuing to pray earnestly and not give up. The parable concerns a widow about to lose everything to a creditor who demanded payment of a debt. She appealed to a judge described as unrighteous, who "didn't fear God or care about men" (Luke 18:4). Lacking compassion, he didn't have the slightest inclination to help another human being.

Of all people in biblical times, a widow was the most vulnerable. She owned nothing, had no rights, and if there was no one to care for her she could be imprisoned in payment for her debts. She came to the judge asking him to "grant her justice against her adversary," make him stop hounding her for debts she could not pay. Luke tells us that the judge refused. But finally he said to himself ... "because this widow keeps bothering me, I will see that she gets justice, so that she won't eventually wear me out with her coming!" (18:5).

Jesus follows the story by teaching us that if even an unrighteous judge will listen to continual pleading, how much more will the all-righteous, all-loving God hear and answer. Verse 8 is key, "I tell you, He will see that they get justice, and quickly. However, when the Son of Man comes, will He find faith on the earth?"

These verses seem to connect to the preceding teaching about Christ's return. Just as the widow never gave up, so Christians must never become discouraged as they wait for the Lord's return. They must persist in prayer for themselves and for others. Unlike the unjust judge, God always does the right thing. It may seem that He delays but from His point of view He acts speedily. Christ will return at just the right time.

Clearly, we're taught to pray and keep on praying. Ours should be no half-hearted, casual or thoughtless utterance, but deep, earnest prayer that recognizes the sovereignty of God and the ultimate reason for our existence—"to act justly and to love mercy and to walk humbly with your God" (Mic. 6:8).

The truth of the parable also applies to any discouraging delays in God's answers. His perfect knowledge surpasses our small sight; we can trust Him, however dark things may look. The more we walk with Him, the more we trust Him and are sustained by His love and promise.

And what if strength should fail,
And heart more deeply bleed?
Or what if dark and lonely days
Draw forth the cry of need?
That cry will bring Thee down
My needy soul to fill,
And Thou wilt teach my yearning heart
To know and do Thy will.

–Fannie Jolliffe, *The Salvation Army Songbook* #586

Chapter 17

PRAYER AT THE END OF THE JOURNEY

"'Lord Jesus, receive my spirit.' Then he knelt down and cried out with a loud voice, 'Lord, do not charge them with this sin.' And when he had said this, he fell asleep"

(Acts 7:59-60).

These were the last words of Stephen who was chosen to wait tables in the early Christian church. An ardent follower of Christ, he never failed to speak for the Lord he loved, but his words so angered the enemies of Christianity that one day they stoned him in the public square. His dying words were hauntingly like those of his beloved Master who, hanging on the cross, forgave his tormentors and died saying, "Father, into Your hands I commit My spirit" (Luke 23:46).

Do you ever wonder what your last words on earth will be?

I sometimes fear that I might die saying something as inane as "please pass the salt," or I might be driving down the street and be remembered as having said, "Not another red light. It's the third one in a row," just before I leave this life.

My husband had always wanted to pass triumphantly into heaven in the midst of giving aid or preaching the Word to some hurting soul, as he'd done for thirty years. His last words after sprinting up a steep hill to our cabin following a game of basketball were, "We won." The next sound was a great cry as his heart succumbed to attack. We all want our final words to have significance, and no one wants to die with anger on our lips.

We tend to avoid thinking about death, even though it's played out in a hundred media hours day and night. My paternal grandmother, who claimed to have no faith at all, used to say, "Thinking about death is a terrible waste of life." But we all knew she thought about it, especially when she would sit in our living room under the portrait of Jesus, a pensive expression on her face. We all think about it, even though we don't want to. After all, we have no control over how we will die. It might be a slow passage or a sudden death at the hands of an enemy. We can't choose that journey; we can only control how we will live and face life's challenges now.

Between Two Eternities

After watching a number of people who have passed away, it seems clear that we die as we have lived. People who live happily and at peace with themselves tend to face death, however quick the passage, in that same attitude. Those who live in denial of God seldom experience any hope in the midst of their deep dread.

When the brother of Robert Ingersoll died, the great atheistic orator decided to preach the graveside service himself rather than call a clergyman. His words reveal the despair that comes from a life lived without faith. "Life," he said, "is a narrow vale between the cold and barren peaks of two eternities. We strive in vain to look beyond the heights. We cry aloud, and the only answer is the echo of our wailing cry."

Ingersoll died as he had lived, without the comfort of knowing he was in God's care. At least, some would say, he died honestly. No last-minute conversion in case he'd been wrong; he was proud and brave to the end.

Ingersoll's contemporary, Dwight L. Moody, who spent his life preaching and teaching a message of hope in Christ, died with his friends and family circling his bed and singing the great hymns of faith. Moody's face, they say, was bright with the reflected glory of the Christ who dwelled within. Moody rejoiced in death as he had rejoiced in life. Both he and Ingersoll died honestly, but only one could be honestly right.

God's Word says that we will all face death, unless the Lord returns to usher in His kingdom first. "It is appointed to man once to die," wrote the author of Hebrews, "and after that the judgment" (9:27). However unpleasant or disconcerting, we can only consider death while we're alive, and what we believe about it will determine how we live, not only in this world but in eternity.

Jesus said, "'I am the resurrection and the life. He who believes in Me, will live even though he dies; and whoever lives and believes in Me will never die'" (John 11:25-26).

Perhaps contemplation about the hereafter may be considered anachronistic in the enlightened and sophisticated 21st century. Even in many churches we are not reminded often enough that there is a heaven to gain and a hell to avoid. Perhaps we are too busy looking for a temporal prosperity we think we're entitled to, rather than seeking God's purpose for us in the eternal now.

Biblical people of faith lived in the certainty that more was involved in this sojourn than sixty or eighty years of making a living on this planet. They believed that God calls us to righteousness and that He "watches over the way of the righteous, but the way of the wicked will perish" (Psalm 1:6). The Apostle Paul never feared coming to the end of the life he had committed to Christ on the Damascus Road. He knew that he would be with his Lord in heaven.

In his epistle to the Corinthians, Paul quotes the psalmist's vibrant hymn of life: "Death swallowed by triumphant life! Who got the last word, oh, Death? Oh, Death, who's afraid of you now? It was sin that made death so frightening" and law–code guilt that gave sin its leverage, its destructive power. But now in a single victorious stroke of Life, all three—sin, guilt, death—are one, the gift of our Master, Jesus Christ. Thank God!" (1 Cor. 15:55-56, *The Message*).

We need have no fear about the final call. We can know that the Lord Jesus will receive us if we have confessed our sin to Him and accepted the salvation He purchased on Calvary. We can have the same confidence that poet Henry Wadsworth Longfellow expressed in his epic poem, "The Building of the Ship:"

Sail on, nor fear to breast the sea!
Our hearts, our hopes, our prayers, our tears,
Our faith triumphant o'er our fears,
Are all with Thee—are all with Thee!

Longfellow died as he lived—in the presence of His Lord. We too lay claim to that astonishing victory.

"Who's got the last word, oh, Death?" Whether or not anyone hears any memorable words to mark our passing, we can know that the single perfect Word has already been spoken, and we will be with Him for all eternity.

Moving Outward Through Prayer

The more we experience God personally, the more we find our arms stretching out to draw others into His fellowship. "Whoever believes in me, as the Scripture has said, streams of living water will flow from within him" (John 7:38). Prayer moves us outward—beyond ourselves—to engage in the life of others, to add to their joy and to embrace their sufferings. God's will for us within the whole community of faith is revealed and we are drawn to pray for others in the light of that will.

Jesus said, "I, when I am lifted up from the earth, will draw all men to Myself" (John 12:32). As we are lifted up and drawn into the divine Center, we will draw others to the Light of the world who dwells in us. What honor and joy to be united with Christ in love for the world and to know that "the prayer of a person living right with God is something powerful to be reckoned with" (James 5:16, *The Message*).

As ripples widen from a pebble thrown into the water, so our witness in the world and our love for others flow far beyond our selves into the lives of others. Nothing is lost in the economy of God, but everything works in concert with His will and purpose like waters flowing out of the ocean into rivers, lakes and tributaries to replenish a thirsty land.

Chapter 18

PRAYER AS INTERCESSION

"Justice is turned back and righteousness stands afar off, for truth is fallen in the street, and equity cannot enter. So truth fails, and he who departs from evil makes himself a prey. Then the Lord saw it, and it displeased Him that there was no justice. He saw that there was no man, and wondered that there was no intercessor" (Isa. 59:14–16 NKJV).

I have often been intrigued by the phrase, "God wondered." To imagine God wondering about anything is disarming, since wonder seems to be ascribed to someone who sees something new or for the first time. Perhaps in this case, the word "wonder" could best be interpreted as "marveled," but the same element of surprise is intrinsic to it. God apparently is amazed or caused to wonder about our lack of appealing to Him in prayer on behalf of each other. I wonder how often we have given God cause to wonder about us in this regard.

A bumper sticker recently sent me exploring again the idea of intercessory prayer. "Pray to stop abortion," the sticker read. Do we need to convince God that abortion is wrong? Do we need to plead with Him to stop something that is most certainly contrary to His will? Does this really change the heart of God—that great heart that has been fixed on mankind in fierce and abiding love from the beginning?

Certainly, He needs no such impetus or reminder. And "God knows what we need even before we ask," Scripture tells us. Yet, we are instructed to pray—not only daily but without ceasing. The reference to intercessory prayer and the effects of it are numerous throughout God's Word. Whole nations were spared because of one righteous man's prayers. We read that Moses intervened for the Israelites whom the Lord described as "stiff-necked." "But Moses sought the favor of the Lord his God. 'O Lord, why should Your anger burn against Your people, whom You brought out of Egypt with great power and a mighty hand? ... Turn from Your fierce anger; relent and do not bring disaster on Your people'" (Exod. 32:11-12). Moses intercedes in a similar vein for the children of Israel in the book of Numbers.

Paul, though called to minister to the Gentiles, had a great heart for his Jewish brothers. "For I could wish that I myself were cursed and cut off from Christ for the sake of my brothers, those of my own race, the people of Israel," he wrote (Rom. 9:3).

The centurion's servant was healed because of the faith of his master (See Luke 7:1-9). Jesus said of this centurion, "I tell you, I have not found such great faith even in Israel" (Luke 7:9) and healed the servant long distance—without even having to touch him.

A young boy was healed based on the faith of his mother. "When the Lord saw her (the widow of Nain whose only son was being carried out dead from the town gate) His heart went out to her." At the word of Jesus the young man "sat up and began to talk, and Jesus gave him back to his mother" (Luke 7:15).

Jesus is our mediator, our great intercessor who even now pleads for us before God. Isaiah tells us that Christ was numbered with the transgressors, bore the sin of many, and made intercession for the transgressors (53:12). Hebrews 7:25 tells us, "He is able to save to the uttermost those who come to God through Him seeing He ever lives to make intercession for them." And can we forget Jesus' high priestly prayer in John 17:9 in which He prayed for His own and for all who would later believe in Him?

One of my earliest recollections was of my mother on her knees in the little sun porch that was her bedroom. All through my childhood and youth, I was aware of her prayers for me and drew comfort and encouragement from them. But no more so than when I became an adult, a mother with my own children. I was certain that mother's prayers kept us alive through the traumas and troubles we experienced. When she passed away, I feared I would be lost without her prayers, that our family would flounder.

I had forgotten that there was One greater than Mother who prayed for me, indeed still prays for me. And we learn in Scripture that Jesus continues at the right hand of the Father to make intercession for us. I often receive letters, phone calls and emails, indicating that someone is praying for me. What empowerment. What grace. But I wonder, how many do I intercede for? What is happening or not happening for good because I have not done so often enough?

Intercession is both an exalting and humbling experience. That God has chosen to work through His people to effect change, and that He allows us to participate in the ongoing process of creation is an astounding privilege. It isn't that He couldn't call out the rocks to testify for Him, but He has chosen that we shall do it. What privilege. What responsibility.

Thus we are taught by precept and example to pray for one another. It is a divine imperative. "Pray continually" (1 Thess. 5:17). Paul exhorted that "requests, prayers, intercession and thanksgiving be made for everyone—for kings and all those in authority, that we may lead peaceful and quiet lives in all godliness and holiness (1 Tim. 2:1-2)."

Intercessory prayer is important, not only because Jesus models and teaches it, but because it moves us to Christian action. It is difficult to harbor bitter feelings or worse yet, apathy, toward a person for whom we are praying. The opposite of love is apathy, disregard. By bringing someone before the divine Love, we ourselves are affected by the radiance of that love and are moved to love the object of our prayers.

Our prayers for each other bind us in community. Dietrich Bonnhoeffer said, "The most direct route to others is prayer." It sensitizes us to one another; and there is great power in the community of saints. Has there ever been a time when the community of faith needed to be bonded together more strongly? We are under attack as at no time in history. More Christians have suffered persecution and martyrdom in the twentieth century than in all the previous centuries put together. We need each other desperately—and a desperate world needs us.

What an honor to participate in the act of creating new persons in Christ, creating wholeness where there is sickness, understanding where there is dissension. We do not need to understand how intercessory prayer works. We need only to pray for one another in obedience and love. There is a wonderful prayer written by Soren Kierkegaard, 19th century theologian and author, that captures the spirit of obedience, even when understanding is lacking:

Teach me, Lord, that the fight of faith is not a fight with doubt, thought against thought, but a fight for character. Enable me to see that human vanity consists in having to understand. Save me from the vanity of not being willing to obey like a child, and of wanting to be like a grown man who has to understand. Help me to realize that he who will not obey when he cannot understand does not, in any essential sense, obey you at all. Make me a believer, a "character man," who, unreservedly obedient, sees it as necessary for his character's sake that he must not always understand. Make me willing to believe even when I cannot understand.

The mandate to pray for one another leads us to the greatest power available in this life. We ignore it to our peril—and the peril of souls God loves.

Chapter 19

FAITH AND HEALING

"Is any among you suffering? Let him pray. Is any cheerful?
Let him sing praise. Is any among you sick? Let him call for
the elders of the church, and let them pray over him, anointing
him with oil in the name of the Lord; and the prayer of faith
will save the sick man, and the Lord will raise him up; and if
he has committed sins, he will be forgiven. Therefore confess
your sins to one another, and pray for one another, that you
may be healed. The prayer of a righteous man has great power
in its effects. Elijah was a man of like nature with ourselves
and he prayed fervently that it might not rain, and for three
years and six months it did not rain on the earth. Then he
prayed again and the heaven gave rain, and the earth brought
forth its fruit" (James 5:13-18 NKJV).

Scripture is replete with references to Christ as Healer. In both testaments, God's power to heal is not only claimed as possible, but demonstrated so frequently that even the most hardened skeptic cannot discount it. There are some, however, who say that healing may have been part of God's program once, but no longer. Though many people have been confused and hurt by deliberate deception about healing, contemporary witnesses testify to God's continued healing ministry.

There may be times when God asks us to rely upon prayer alone for healing, but this is the exception, not the rule. The refusal to use medical means to promote healing may be a gesture of faith—but more often it is a gesture of spiritual pride.

We can make a mistake in the other direction too. Many trust in medical means exclusively and turn to prayer only when all available medical technology has failed. This betrays the materialistic base of so much of our thinking. Prayer and the aid of medicine should be pursued at the same time and with equal vigor, for both are gifts from God.

In his book *The Blood and Fire in Canada*, R.G. Moyles points out that Catherine Booth was a strong proponent of "faith–healing." She wrote about its practices in early editions of *The War Cry*, and there were occasional testimonies to the good effect of faith-healing services. It seemed for a while that this would become one of the Army's key beliefs. Eventually, it was abandoned both in practice and publications.

In a major directive on faith healing issued in 1902, General William Booth wrote:

That God should heal the sick after this fashion (faith or divine healing) is in perfect harmony with the views and experience of The Salvation Army from the beginning. Nothing to the contrary has ever been taught by our authority, and numerous instances of faith-healing have occurred in the Army throughout its history.

I do not believe there can be a corps ... at home or abroad ... in which some signs and wonders have not been wrought. Have we not seen men and women and little children raised up from the borders of the grave, and restored to health and vigor, in answer to the prayer of faith?

But views have been set forth outside our ranks on the subject of faith healing that are false, misleading and ruinous.

It must not be taught that Jesus Christ has, by His atoning sacrifice, redeemed the body as He has redeemed the soul. Or in other words, that he has procured health for the body in this life in the same sense that he procured salvation for the soul. ... It must not be taught amongst us that those who exercise faith in God for healing are cured when there is evidence that they are not.

These notions must not be taught for although there is little ground for fear of permanent loss there are always some of the weaker sort who will be in danger of being turned out of the way. Moreover, there is a class who are more readily carried off by the idea of signs and wonders (see Faith Healing, A Memorandum).

Booth deliberately distanced the Army from the Pentecostal belief that healing is in the atonement, and that physical healing in this life is a right for the Christian. This further set the Army on a path that would lead it to diverge from the direction taken by charismatics in later years. Fearful of excesses and imbalance, it steered away from what seemed an uncontrolled movement of the Spirit. It could be suggested that the freedom and joy in the Spirit that once characterized The Salvation Army is now largely absent, though the worship choruses from the charismatic movement are being widely used in our services.

Colonel Max Ryan comments in the Canadian journal *Past and Present*: "It remains to be seen whether a younger generation of Salvation Army leaders will reflect on the denomination's roots and once again welcome the refreshing winds of the Spirit to a denomination that a number of Salvationists think has lost its way by becoming too stuffy and rigid."

It would be sad, and unfaithful to human experience, to say that God no longer heals and to limit by our fear God's work in our bodies, minds and emotions as well as our souls. Medical authorities do not discount the importance of faith in healing the body. There is no lack of written statement to that effect in today's journals and documentaries.

Many of us have our personal stories of healing through prayer. My husband's grandfather, who was known for his "hallelujah dances," (particularly his singing of the old Salvation Army ballad, "Where Did You Get That Hat?" as he performed in the open air ring) testified to complete and instantaneous healing from diabetes. His healing was later corroborated by his doctor, and he lived to perform many a "hallelujah dance."

When our son was born, doctors warned that he was not likely to live long enough to reach his first birthday, and if he did live beyond that he would demand a heavy financial and emotional toll on our family. Born with congenital lung disease, that resulted in frequent pneumonia and other diseases, he spent more time in the hospital than out during childhood. Each time a new problem arose, we would commit him to God through both medical assistance and prayer—oh, so fervent, often desperate prayer. God was faithful and showed His love and healing power over the years in a variety of ways.

An operation for the removal of the lung brought relief from the continual bouts of pneumonia, but he struggled with a fragile breathing system. We used to know our son was still alive each time we stepped out of the elevator onto the hospital floor because we could hear his labored, rasping breathing. Twice before he reached his teen years, he was placed on a respirator. He was even baptized without our knowledge in a Catholic hospital because they were sure he wouldn't live until morning.

There were long nights of waiting in prayer. Once, a hospital chaplain came to sit with us, occasionally whispering a prayer, but most of the time waiting in silence with us. What courage he inspired. We later learned that the chaplain of the hospital was not on duty that night and no replacement had been arranged. The hospital staff had never heard of the man who sat with us or knew how to get in touch with him. Our son not only lived until morning; he was released two days later.

Though God healed him completely from asthma, an ailment he endured for eight years, this would not be the end of his suffering. At age 16, spinal surgery was necessary to stop the growth of the spine toward the vacuum created by the missing lung. He would experience months of recuperation, including nine months in a full body cast. Once more we clung God's healing and sustaining grace.

The night before surgery was to be performed, a saintly retired Salvation Army officer in Houston, Texas came to visit. He brought a little vial of oil and touched a drop on my son's forehead and prayed for him. How that encouraged us. How sacred to feel the presence of Christ in that room—not because of any special substances or rituals—but because the Lord's spirit surrounded us.

Through faith and remarkable breakthroughs in modern medicine, our son lived 37 years, knowing the strong presence of Christ. In 2001, he went home to be with the Lord and to his total healing. His earthly life was a ministry of patient suffering and reliance on God's grace. He developed a sparkling humor and a loving heart in the midst of these experiences—an outcome that only the presence of Christ in his life could bring about.

Can we know all the answers, the reasons for suffering? Who can know but God who is Answer enough to all our needs and who is the great Healer of bodies and souls? As William Booth stated in his *Memorandum of Faith Healing,* "God is the First Great Cause ... the Healer behind all influences and means." Sometimes His healing is instantaneous; other times it is gradual or completed only after release from this world. God chooses, and always His choice is the right one.

Chapter 20

A PRAYER OF SALVATION

"Abraham approached him and said: "Will You sweep away the righteous with the wicked? What if there are fifty righteous people in the city? Will You really sweep it away and not spare the place for the sake of the fifty righteous people in it? … Will not the Judge of all the earth do right?"

(Gen. 18:22–25).

At first glance, this would seem an impertinent prayer. Moses appears to be bargaining with the God of the universe, suggesting to Him that if He continued on His planned course to destroy Sodom and Gomorrah, He would not be right in His actions.

As the account continues, we find Abraham pleading with God until God agrees to spare the cities if only ten righteous persons could be found within its boundaries. "'For the sake of ten, I will not destroy it.' When the Lord had finished speaking with Abraham, he left, and Abraham returned home" (Gen. 18:32–33).

Actually only one person of dubious righteousness was found, and Lot was spared though the city was not. The account seems to portray Abraham as more compassionate than God. Well, that is the limited human view. But God's ultimate purpose with Abraham–as it is with all of us—was to reveal Himself: "Shall I hide from Abraham what I am about to do?" the Lord asks. "Abraham will surely become a great and powerful nation, and all the nations on earth will be blessed through him" (18:17-18).

God's Plan for All to Be Saved

Through this incident Abraham learned something about God's patience and compassion. God revealed His plan to destroy the two wicked cities because of their grave sin (sin that if left unchecked could have kept Abraham's descendants and all the children of Israel from fulfilling His righteous plan for all mankind. But the account shows that almost any excuse is enough for God to refrain from exercising His justified wrath. "The Lord is compassionate and gracious, slow to anger, abounding in love" (Psalms 103:8). God all but asks Abraham to intercede for Sodom and Gomorrah, even as He pleads with you and me to intercede for others who are likewise perishing during our lifetime.

"God is not willing that any should perish." His unchanging plan for the whole world is that it be reconciled to Himself, but continued refusal to turn from sin will make it impossible for those in rebellion to be saved. He invites you and me to participate in His plan to redeem the world through intercession.

God's plan included the destruction of Sodom and Gomorrah, though it grieved Him to do this. The exchange with His servant Abraham seems to imply that His action could change if ten righteous persons could be found.

Does God Change His Mind?

God affirms, "I the Lord do not change" (Matt. 3:6). Scripture and our Christian doctrine teach the immutability or unchangeableness of God. How reassuring down through the ages to know that though everything else changes, God does not. So when we read that the Lord "was grieved" or "repented" about something He has done or planned, we are caught off guard. How can this be? God's unchangeableness on one hand, his invitation to intercede with Him to change on the other?

The point is not that God has changed in His character or in what He stands for. Instead, a human term is used to refer to a perfectly good and necessary divine action. When the Bible says that God repented, the idea is that His feelings toward some person or group changed in response to some action on the part of the objects of His action or some mediator who intervened (often by God's own direction and plan). Often in the very same passages that announce God's repentance there is a firm denial of any alteration in God's plan, purpose or character.

1 Samuel 15:29 reminds us that "the Glory of Israel does not lie or change His mind; for He is not a man that He should change His mind." Yet Samuel made that statement the day after the Lord told him that He was grieved over making Saul king (1 Sam. 15:11).

From our human perspective, it appears that the use of the word "grieved" indicates that God changed His purpose. But the expression when used of God is anthropopathic (a description of our Lord in terms of human emotions and passions).

The point is that unchangeableness must not be thought of as if it were some type of frozen immobility. God is not some impervious being who cannot respond when circumstances or individuals change. Rather, he is a living person, and as such He can and does change when the occasion demands it. He does not change in His character, person or plan. But He can and does respond to <u>our</u> changes.

The Lord of the Harvest

Thus, Jesus urged His disciples to "pray the Lord of the harvest to send out laborers into His harvest" (Matt. 9:38). His harvest is the souls of men and women for whom He died. He longs to save them, to bring them into relationship with Himself, but because He has limited Himself to our willingness to accept Him, He can save only those who come to God by Him.

He has chosen that you and I intercede for them—through our prayers and the actions that prove or prayers are earnest. He implores us to reach out to those who have not accepted Him, to lovingly influence them, draw them, to literally "snatch them from the flames" (Jude 22).

Our prayers make a difference, not only for ourselves (growing ever nearer to God through relationship), but also for others who need that same relationship with the One who loves them with an everlasting love. Indeed, His unquenchable love is what persuades Him to hold back His hand of judgment on an unbelieving world.

"The Lord is not slow in keeping His promise," we read in 2 Peter 3:9. "He is patient with you, not wanting anyone to perish, but everyone to come to repentance." What honor and privilege to align ourselves with the unchanging purpose of God to save us all and to know that our prayers matter. Indeed, intercession for someone else could make the most profound change of all in that life.

Chapter 21

A Pastor's Prayer for His Church

"And this is my prayer: that your love may abound more and more in knowledge and depth of insight, so that you may be able to discern what is best and may be pure and blameless until the day of Christ, filled with the fruit of righteousness that comes through Jesus Christ to the glory and praise of God" (Phil. 1:9-11).

Ever wonder what God and your pastor talk about in prayer? If you are part of a local church where God's Word is honored, you can be certain that you are included in that special conversation. It is the pastor's duty to pray for you. God holds His shepherd accountable.

Paul's prayer serves as a model of deep love and earnest longing. "In all my prayers for all of you, I always pray with joy," Paul writes (Phil. 1:3). Surely the faces of his dear friends were imbedded in his mind as he prayed. Philippi was special to Paul, and for good reason. It was the gateway to the Gentiles where the first converts in Europe were won to Christ.

When he arrived in Philippi, Paul found no synagogue, so he began his ministry in an outdoor service by a riverside. Among his converts were Lydia, a successful merchant, a slave girl with magical powers and a jailer ready to kill himself because he feared he had failed in his duty. Paul came to know each one personally as he led them into a relationship with Jesus, and they became his "sons and daughters" in the Lord.

"I thank my God every time I remember you," Paul wrote from prison where he was later incarcerated for preaching the gospel. He yearned for the faith of the Philippians to grow in three specific areas:

A Tender and Growing Love

He prayed that they would "abound in love"—the identifying mark of the Christian, as outlined in Galatians 5:22. Imagine what would happen if each of us was full of love, as God intends for us to be, and that our love would expand to take in every other soul we met. Would there be rifts and dissensions among the people of God? How sad that the very people who should exude holy care and friendship often display a deplorable lack of love.

"Dear friends, let us love one another, for love comes from God," wrote the Apostle John. "Whoever does not love does not know God, because God is love" (1 John 4:7–8). Nothing could be clearer. We show that we are truly children of God by our love for Him and others. How much we need to pray this prayer. The kind of love that comes from God is far removed from sentimental feeling or an affection that comes and goes as moods dictate.

Canon Tallis suggests that for our day the best translation of "love" is the name of Jesus. That name will tell us everything about love we need to know. God is always calling us to be more than we are, to see through the sham to the real, to break down our defenses in order to be free to give and receive love.

Lawrence Cunningham writes, "It may be necessary to give up warm and fuzzy religious feelings, or have them taken from us by God to draw closer to the One who first comes to us in darkness, but who ultimately is revealed, as John writes, as a living flame of love." Only as we spend time with our Lord in daily prayer and listen to the voice of His Holy Spirit within us will we grow in Christ—in love.

While God's love is infused in our hearts the moment we accept Jesus Christ as Savior, it is not a static, full blown reality in our lives immediately. Scripture tells us to "walk in love." As we daily experience Christ, and He motivates our thought and actions, love for Him and for those He loves will grow and deepen.

A Pursuit of Excellence

Paul prays that the Christians in Philippi would grow in knowledge and discernment, so that they make right choices in their lives. Without sound judgment in applying God's truth in every situation of life, love becomes a mere unguided emotion.

Paul writes in a later chapter of the same epistle that we grow in our faith by meditating on things that are "true, noble, right, pure, lovely, and admirable. Where can these virtues be found? And how will we recognize them when they do appear?

Information explodes all around us that can be downloaded in an instant in ever better and faster media. We all move on a superhighway of information that seems at times to overwhelm the hardiest constitution. But is this information sound and true and enduring? Is it excellent? Does it lead to wisdom—the holy wisdom that is found in Christ alone?

We will need fresh allegiance to prayer and obedience if we are to achieve excellence or holy wisdom as God requires it. We will need to carve out time be alone with Him. A prayer written by John Oxenham in the 19th century remains uncommonly pertinent for our age:

Mid all the traffic of the ways, /Turmoils without, within, /Make in my heart a quiet place, And come and dwell therein: A little shrine of quietness,/ All sacred to Thyself, / Where Thou shalt all my soul possess, /And I may find myself.

A Treasured Purity

Finally, Paul prays that the Church will be "pure and blameless ... filled with the fruit of righteousness that comes through Jesus Christ" (1:9). If our most ardent and frequent thoughts were prayers, we might be asking God to make us successful, prosperous, respected. Aren't these the qualities that most people aspire to? But our treasures, as God's redeemed people, are treasures of the spirit that will endure for eternity.

"Do not store up for yourselves treasures on earth, where moth and rust destroy," said Jesus, "... But store up for yourselves treasures in heaven ... For where your treasure is, there your heart will be also" (Matt. 6:19-21). The prayer of Paul for righteousness should be our prayer as well. Jesus instructed, "Seek first His kingdom and His righteousness, and all these things will be given to you as well" (Matt. 6:33).

The pastor's prayer to grow in love, excellence and purity should be our personal prayer as well, and our plea for all brothers and sisters in Christ. A dying world depends on us. As "adjectives always pointing to the noun of truth," our daily activities in the world may spell the difference between death and life for someone else.

Chapter 22

PRAYER FOR A DECLINING CULTURE

"Help, Lord, for the godly are no more" (Psalm 12:1).

A shocking story was reported on national television. A woman admitted to throwing her baby out of a car window onto a busy highway. Perhaps we have heard so many shocking stories that nothing surprises us, but this story reaches a new level of horror. How could a member of the human race—our race—do this? The story turned out to be a hoax—a lie to cover up the true story of how she had disposed of her baby. The lie somehow made the deed even more ghastly.

In the flood of evil reported daily we often feel as though we're lost in a wilderness with no hope of reaching civilization. We cry with the Psalmist, "Help, Lord, for the godly are no more." We struggle with the sense that there are no more good people. Everyone lies, the Psalmist laments, "Their flattering lips speak with deception" (Psalm 12:1). We are reminded of the old Billy Joel song: "Honesty, it's such a lonely word. Everyone is so untrue."

Of course, the reality is that not everyone has breached integrity with lies. When a despairing Elijah was running for his life from Jezebel who dogged him with blood in her eye, he asked the Lord to take his life. "I'm the only one left who is righteous," he complained. But God reminded him that there were 7,000 people in Israel who had not bowed their knees to Baal, the false god of the Canaanites (1 Kings 19:18). With this clarification, God told Elijah to get up off the ground, quit crying and do the work he was called to do.

A Matter of the Heart

The Psalmist decries "idle words, flattering lips, and tongues that speak proud things" and contrasts them with "pure words, like silver tried in a furnace of the earth, purified seven times" (Psalm 12:6). Why does the Psalmist put so much emphasis on evil speaking? He knows that not only do words have tremendous power, but that what is inside of us comes out in what we say. The real terror is in the heart of a person. Jesus said,

"The good man brings good things out of the good stored up in him, and the evil man brings evil things out of the evil stored up in him" (Matt. 12:35).

Mankind left to itself is doomed to all sorts of evil speech, thought and action. God's Word says, "There is no one righteous, not even one" (Rom. 3:10). Without divine intervention we are without hope and find ourselves, in the words of the Apostle John, "wretched, pitiful, poor, blind and naked" (Rev. 3:17). Once we recognize our need of God and call out for help, He is swift to respond, as the Psalmist notes: "'Because of the oppression of the weak and the groaning of the needy, I will now arise,' says the Lord; 'I will protect them from those who malign them'" (Psalms 12:5). The Psalmist moves on from personal complaint over his environment to God's gracious promise to help those who depend on Him. He confirms that the Lord will "protect them ... forever" (12:7).

A Double Promise

Yes, we live in the midst of a declining culture, a milieu in which wicked people seem to prosper. We who are trying to do what is right are often maligned and oppressed. We are reminded that in the 20th century more Christians have been martyred for their faith than in all the centuries preceding it. But God's promise remains. He withholds His righteous judgment because of His great compassion. His arms reach out to save even those who seem beyond help. He hears our "groaning" and promises to protect us.

The promise is one of salvation for those who repent and turn to Him. It is also an assurance that while we live in an idolatrous age, we will one day have the "safety for which (we) yearn" (12:5). We are the minority that dares to go against the grain of society and do what is right, rather than what is politically or socially correct. We will be persecuted for our stance. Jesus said this would be the case: "In this world you will have trouble, but take heart! I have overcome the world" (John 16:33).

He promises to sustain us and keep us upright in the midst of this world's modern chaos. We do well to remember that we don't travel through this wilderness alone. Even as God reminded Elijah, He reminds us that there are Christians everywhere today—some who will bravely make the ultimate sacrifice for faith—and we can be encouraged.

A Godly Mandate

God directed Elijah to "go ... return on your way to the wilderness" (1 Kings 1:15). The Psalmist calls the righteous to honor what is right and refuse to let evil go unchecked. "The wicked freely strut about when what is vile is honored among men," he writes (12:8). When there is no disapproval voiced, wickedness flourishes.

Evil is often paraded as something to be valued, something wiser or more sophisticated than the outmoded conventions of an earlier era. Jesus warned us that one of the signs of the end times would be a strong delusion in which people, unable to tell wrong from right, would call darkness light and light darkness.

"For false Christs and false prophets will appear and perform great signs and miracles to deceive even the elect—if that were possible" (Matt. 24:24). We must be clear about what is right and what is wrong. Without the Holy Spirit's guidance, we are in danger of being fooled, but He has promised to help us discern the truth from the lie. Then knowing what is right, our task is to promote it and to denounce what is clearly wrong, remembering, "All that is necessary for the triumph of evil is that good men do nothing" (Edmund Burke). The Psalmist urges us to "return to the wilderness," to actively fight against wrong doing wherever it is found and live the truth of God.

"Help, Lord, for the godly are no more," we cry. And He responds with His timeless message of hope and salvation and bids us to help those who are dying of thirst in the wilderness. In a declining culture, we shine as lights—reflecting the only hope for us all.

Chapter 23

THE PRAYER OF SELF-FORGETTING LOVE

"Father, forgive them for they do not know what they do"

(Luke 23:34)

This prayer stands as the greatest example of self–forgetting love in all of Scripture and human history. Some followers of Jesus would demonstrate this same love down to their last breath. As an angry mob pelted him with stones and Saul of Tarsus held the coats of the pious murderers, Stephen prayed for the forgiveness of those who were killing him. Saul would later say—after being transformed into the Apostle Paul by the amazing grace of God—that he would be willing to be damned forever if only his countrymen could be saved (see Rom. 9:3).

Stephen and Paul and other saints reached this pinnacle of self–forgetting love through prayer—that divine umbilical cord that nourishes the spirit with the supernatural love of God. These men and women responded from God–bent hearts to the greatest love ever witnessed.

Jesus' prayer from the cross is amazing from both divine and human perspectives. Consider that He was the Son of the Almighty God who had spoken the world into being, who governs all things, who could call a host of angels to do His bidding. And consider that He suffered the most ignoble, inhuman death that men could devise. Death by crucifixion suffocated its victims slowly as the weight of the body hanging from the spikes choked off air to the brain and lungs. Christ, already crushed and bleeding from the merciless floggings He endured, hung for hours in agony. Yet, from this posture of pain came His words of forgiveness. What dignity. What love.

"There is dignity in suffering," said Cardinal Theodore McCarrick, Archbishop of Washington, D.C., in a televised speech as Pope John Paul II lay dying while 70,000 people in the Vatican's St. Peter's Square kept vigil. Like his Lord, the Pope would not "go gently into that good night," as poet Thomas Dylan wrote. He clung to life, every precious moment of it, and in his dying wanted to remain connected to the people. He wanted to give open evidence to his belief in the sanctity of human life—every human life.

Even a life of suffering is a life of dignity if we suffer in the spirit of Christ. Those who preach a doctrine of death with dignity might well have robbed the world of the greatest gift it ever received. They might have demanded that Christ be quickly euthanized—or even had Him shot on the cross—to put Him out of His misery—as though He were a dying horse rather than the Son of God.

No man ever displayed more nobility, more dignity, more love than Jesus did in His suffering. He was dying to preserve life for every man, conquering the greatest enemy and swallowing it up in His victory. "O Death, where is your sting? O Hades, where is your victory? ... But thanks be to God, who gives us the victory through our Lord Jesus Christ" (1 Cor. 15:55-57).

A life lived in the spirit of the Life–giver is of great worth, even if those looking on can see no purpose in it. Many, including her husband, saw no reason for Terri Shaivo to go on being sustained by a feeding tube. He had the life-sustaining device removed in this now famous "right to die" case. Terri Shaivo's fifteen years in what some would say was a worthless state—a life of no quality—were lived bravely revealing a dignity in suffering that even the pundits of "good death" cannot deny.

"When you do good and suffer, if you take it patiently, this is commendable before God," wrote the Apostle Peter. "For to this you were called, because Christ also suffered for us, leaving us an example, that you should follow His steps ... who, when He suffered ... committed Himself to Him who judges righteously" (1 Pet. 2:20-23).

Indeed, who else is qualified to judge with perfect righteousness? Ours is only to follow the Life–giver who values every life and endows it with His own righteous purpose.

The longer we live in communion with God, the more we become like our suffering Lord who wastes nothing; not our tears or our suffering or our joys. All the experiences He allows into our lives work toward a purpose that He has designed. Some sneer at this promise in Scripture, but it remains unchanged and unalterable: "All things work together for good to those who love God, to those who are called according to His purpose" (Rom. 8:28).

That He uses ordinary people to fulfil His gracious design is only too obvious in our own lives. We were reminded of this truth again through the life of the young woman who was abducted by a murderer. She was no "great saint" by human standards but was diligently seeking God. Through prayer and bravery only God could supply she was able to subdue her kidnapper, to get him to listen and think about what he was doing as he kept her captive at gunpoint in a motel in Atlanta. What Ashley Smith read were the words of another ordinary human being who wrote a powerful book. We heard on national television how *The Purpose-Driven Life* by Rick Warren was used to turn around a potential catastrophe. When escaped felon Brian Nichols submitted himself voluntarily to the authorities without harming her, it was without doubt the result of God's divine hand working through the living prayers of His people.

As we live in Him, directed by His Holy Spirit, we fulfill His purpose for us. It doesn't matter whether we can see the design He is creating. Perhaps we see only a thread here and there, or a fuzzy outline like the underside of a work of embroidery. He who created us is weaving a masterpiece. It's our job to remain open to Him and allow His work of love to be done in us.

Perhaps, like me, you look at yourself and wonder if you will ever reach such a pinnacle—the self–forgetting love of Jesus. Perhaps you are passing through an illness or a difficulty in which you see nothing positive, useful or redeeming. At one time, Peter was so imperiled, so fearful and self–conscious that he denied Christ with a curse. But he repented and began following again—closer and closer—until he became a powerful witness for God, eventually giving his own life as a martyr because of love for God. The Roman authorities ordered that Peter be hung on a cross, like his Master, but he asked to be hung upside down, because he considered himself unworthy to die the same death as Jesus.

Are we willing to become like Jesus even if we are in a dark place that seems to have no reason or rhyme? Like the saint of old do we whisper, "Oh to live in Him, invisible and dim"? Do we, like Paul long "to know Him and the power of His resurrection and the fellowship of His sufferings" (Phil. 3:10)? If we do, we will have found the great purpose for our lives.

Let this prayer by Evelyn Underhill be our prayer as well:

Come! Spirit of Love! Penetrate and transform us by the action of Your purifying life. May Your constant, brooding love bring forth in us more love and all the graces and works of love. Give us grace to remain still under its action, and may that humble stillness be our prayer. Amen.

Chapter 24

THE CONTINUING RELEVANCE
OF PRAYER

"I have held many things in my hands, and lost them all.

But whatever I put in God's hands, that I still possess."

This is the picture of prevailing prayer. By putting our desires

in His hands, we possess His blessings. And while the path

up Prayer Mountain may be steep and tiring, it's often God's

way of strengthening us to receive His answer. God has

commanded persevering prayer. His answer may not come

within our timetable; but His answers are always on time

and always right.

—Martin Luther

We learn something of persevering prayer through Elijah's confrontation with the prophets of Baal on Mt. Carmel. Elijah's weary servant stayed with his master after the crowds had all gone home. The drama of the contest was over. Weak from cutting themselves and screaming to their god, the prophets of Baal were still. The smoke from the massive sacrifices was all but dissipated. It remained for the promise of rain to be realized, according to the word of Elijah.

Elijah had prayed for the rain God had withheld because of the wickedness of the people. After some time Elijah called out to his servant to go up the steep rocky trail at the base of the mountain and look toward the sea. Six times Elijah ordered the servant up the hill with the same instruction. After being ordered up the mountain for the seventh time, the servant's patience had been stretched to the limit, but he plodded once more up the path. Perhaps he did not expect anything. He narrowed his eyes in sudden amazement. "I see a cloud as small as a man's hand," he whispered.

It took seven trips before the first glimpse of answered prayer was seen. We are not told how long each trip up the mountain took, but we can be assured that in those days of difficult travel, the time period was significant.

We're often like that servant in our own prayer life. We don't mind going up the steep path of prayer once or twice, but then our hope begins to falter. We want our answer immediately, and often when we don't see any change right away, we resist going back to pray again.

A parable in Luke 11: 5-8 illustrates perseverance in prayer. It concerns a man who was asked to help a neighbor late at night. He was unwilling to get up out of his warm bed, rouse his family and help his neighbor, but eventually, he did get up—not because he was a man of great compassion, but because he wanted the neighbor to go away.

Jesus applied a spiritual lesson to this story. "I tell you, though he will not get up and give to him the bread because he is his friend, yet because of the man's boldness he will get up and give him as much as he needs" (Luke 11:8). Then comes the monumental truth. Jesus says, "Ask, and it will be given to you; seek and you will find; knock, and the door will be opened to you. For everyone who asks receives; and he who seeks finds; and to him who knocks the door will be opened" (11:9-10). The essence of these imperatives from a Greek perspective is that we keep on asking, keep on seeking, keep on knocking and God will honor our persistent requests.

Another parable in Luke 18 concerns a widow who kept showing up in court to plead her case. The godless judge, tired of her continual pleas, finally ruled that justice be restored to her. The judge in the first parable was not shown to be a loving individual and the judge in the second was described as "godless." What could these individuals have in common with a God who longs to give good gifts to His beloved children?

It was the judge's choice in each case to delay a response, even as God sometimes delays His responses to us. The judge delayed out of selfish indifference; God often delays His responses out of love. We know from Scripture that He works out all things for our good, so that even when we can't see anything good in God's silences, we can be sure that God has a reason for waiting to give us what we ask for.

God calls us to "ask, to seek, to knock" and not give up. The very act of persisting in prayer helps us to learn to praise Him as the sovereign Lord, not as a divine vending machine. Remember that the purpose of prayer is relationship. He knows what we need for the development of our relationship with Him. He knows what will satisfy us for eternity, and that can only be the gift of Himself. It is a gift that often takes us a long time to unwrap.

Since we are assured that God wants to answer our prayers and that He loves us with infinite love, we must concede that there could be reasons why God delays His answer. We may need to deal with parts of our lives that are displeasing to God. The Bible records more than fifty times when God didn't answer someone's prayer; most were due to sin. Consider Saul who took charge of the battle offering—the sacrifice that should only have been offered by the priest. Saul added to his sin by seeking counsel from a medium. In consequence, Saul's prayers were blocked by disobedience.

David, Saul's successor, declared, "If I had cherished sin in my heart, the Lord would not have listened" (Psalm 66:18). Jesus tells us that we should not pray if we have an unresolved conflict with someone. "If you are offering your gift at the altar and there remember that your brother has something against you, leave your gift there in front of the altar. First go and be reconciled to your brother; and then come and offer your gift" (Matt. 5:23-24).

James 4:3 pin-points self–indulgence as a barrier: "When you ask, you do not receive, because you ask with wrong motives, that you may spend what you get on your pleasures." Husbands who dishonor their wives and vice versa will be hindered in prayer according to 1 Peter 3:7. "Live with your wives and treat them with respect ... as heirs with you of the gracious gift of life so that nothing will hinder your prayers."

If God delays responding to our prayers, it might be that He is waiting for growth in our lives before He answers. Habakkuk couldn't understand why God was punishing his people by allowing a pagan nation to conquer them. But Habakkuk admitted growth in his spiritual perspective after he had listened to God declare His holiness and justice. "You're in control, Lord. Even though the world is falling apart, I will still rejoice in You" (Hab. 3:18, *The Message*).

God may delay or say "no" in order to engineer a total answer. For hundreds of years the Israelites prayed for their Messiah, but He came "in the fullness of time," not before. And God is the One who chooses when the time is right for something to happen.

Corrie ten Boom prayed that her sister would be healed at Ravensbruck, a World War II German concentration camp where they both were imprisoned for hiding German refugees while in Holland. Instead, her sister died. When Corrie was released she learned that her sister, had she lived, would have had to remain in the concentration camp without her. "I have praised and thanked my Lord for that unanswered prayer," she said. " Just imagine if she had been healed and would have had to stay in that hell of Ravensbruck without me. I would have returned to my homeland tormented night and day by the consciousness of her suffering. I saw God's side of the embroidery."

In this case, God's no resulted in a worldwide ministry of grace and forgiveness. God may delay His answer to teach us the wisdom of His silence. "My thoughts are not your thoughts, neither are your ways My ways," (Isaiah 55:8). Sometimes we may not know the outcome of an answered prayer until we set foot in Heaven. Then we'll know that it was answered, but not in ways we understood at the time of our prayer.

Jesus taught us to pray and to keep on praying. He taught that God knows what we need but that He waits for us to spend time with Him, to learn from Him, to grow like Him, to enjoy His fellowship. We do not know how much longer we have before God will wrap up the world like a garment no longer needed. When He does, He will take us to be with Him—children of His heart clothed in His righteousness.

After the parable of the persistent widow in Luke's gospel, we are faced with a haunting question: "When the Son of Man comes, will He really find faith on the earth?" We can give the answer He waits to hear if by our daily practice of prayer we say to our Lord, "By Your grace, You will find me faithful."

As we fellowship with Him, our inner resources grow richer, stronger, and our love to others reflects the divine love working in us through prayer. Will we ever exhaust its riches? After forty years of ministry and learning at the feet of Jesus, I sometimes feel as though I've barely scratched the surface. Oh, "the incomparable riches of His grace, expressed in His kindness to us in Christ Jesus" (Eph. 2:7).

How prayer works has kept theologians and seeking saints wondering for centuries. Wondering yet certain that like God whose greatness is so immense, so unlimited we cannot plumb its depths, prayer remains a mystery—a powerful, enabler, a preserving reality that will never be exhausted.

O Thou by whom we come to God,
The life, the truth, the way!
The path of prayer Thyself hast trod;
Lord, teach us how to pray!
(James Montgomery, The Salvation Army Song Book # 615)

Appendix

PRAYERS AS WE LOOK UPWARD

These prayers, chosen from a variety of texts, ancient and contemporary, focus on intimacy with God. They express our love and adoration of Him. Along with prayers of your own, these expressions can help you as you continue in a life of prayer.

Song of Praise from Revelation

Jesus, You are worthy to take the scroll and to open its seals, because You were slain, and with Your blood You purchased men for God from every tribe and language and people and nation. You have made them to be a kingdom and priests to serve our God, and they will reign on the earth ...Worthy is the Lamb, who was slain, to receive power and wealth and wisdom and strength and honor and glory and praise! ... To Him who sits on the throne and to the Lamb be praise and honor and glory and power for ever and ever! Amen.

—Revelation 5:9-13.

Speak, Lord, For Your Servant is Listening

Speak, Lord, for Your servant is listening. Incline my heart to Your words, and let Your speech come upon me as dew upon the grass.

In days gone by the children of Israel said to Moses, Speak to us and we shall listen; do not let the Lord speak to us, lest we die." This is not how I pray, Lord. No. With the great prophet Samuel, I humbly and earnestly beg: Speak Lord, for your servant is listening."

So, do not let Moses speak to me, but You, O Lord, my God, eternal Truth, You speak to me. If I hear Your voice, may I not be condemned for hearing the word and not following it, for knowing it and not loving it, for believing it and not living it. Speak then, Lord, for Your servant listens, for You have the words of eternal life. Speak to me to comfort my soul and to change my whole life; in turn, may it give You praise and glory and honor, forever and ever. Amen.

—Thomas a' Kempis

I Have Only Today
My life is an instant,
An hour which passes by;
My life is a moment
Which I have no power to stay.
You know, O my God,
That to love You here on earth—
I have only today.

—Theresa of Lisieux

As the Deer Pants
As the deer pants for streams of water,
So my soul pants for You, O God.
My soul thirsts for God, for the living God.

—Psalm 42:1-2

A Prayer of Ecstasy
Fire.
God of Abraham, God of Isaac, God of Jacob,
Not of the philosophers and scholars.
Certitude.
Certitude.
Feeling.
Joy.
Peace.
God of Jesus Christ.
Forgetfulness of the world and of everything, except God.
Greatness of the Human Soul.
Joy, joy, joy, tears of joy.

—Blaise Pascal

(Pascal notes that this experience happened to him on Monday, Nov. 23, 1654, from about half past ten in the evening until about half past twelve. He sewed this prayer into the lining of his coat so that it would always be with him.)

Deeply Cleanse

Come, Holy Spirit, and deeply cleanse; fill us with Yourself. Take away even the desire and tendency to sin. Make us clean, pure, a place where You are comfortable in taking up residence."

—Commissioner Israel Gaither in *My Father, Our Father*

A Prayer of David

Hear, O Lord, and answer me,
For I am poor and needy.
Guard my life, for I am devoted to you.
You are my God; save your servant
Who trusts in you.
Have mercy on me, O Lord,
For I call to you all day long.
Bring joy to your servant,
For to you, O Lord, I lift up my soul.

—Psalm 86: 1-4

Trust in God

Though Thy waves and billows are gone o'er me,
Night and day my meat has been my tears,
Fain I would pour out my soul before Thee,
At whose hand my advocate appears.
Only Thou art still my soul's defender.
Hand of strength, and all-prevenient grace;
Frail am I, but Thou art my befriender.
And I trust the shining of Thy face,

—General Albert Orsborn, *The Salvation Army Songbook* 762

Prayers as We Look Inward

These prayers focus on the transformation of the human personality. As you read them and form your own expressions, ask God to search your heart, to penetrate your mind and help you to see yourself as He sees you.

Enlighten the Darkness of my Heart

O most high, glorious God, enlighten the darkness of my heart and give me A right faith, a certain hope and a perfect love, understanding and knowledge, O Lord, that I may carry out your holy and true command.

—Francis of Assisi

Search me, O God, and know my heart; test me and know my thoughts. See if there is any offensive way in me, and lead me in the way everlasting.

—Psalm 139: 23, 24

The Serenity Prayer

God, grant us the serenity to accept the things we cannot change, courage to change the things we can, and wisdom to know the difference. Amen.

—Reinhold Niebuhr

Be Pleased to Cleanse Me

O Lord, I have heard a good word inviting me to look away to Thee and be satisfied. My heart longs to respond, but sin has clouded my vision till I see Thee but dimly. Be pleased to cleanse me in Thine own precious blood, and make me inwardly pure, so that I may with unveiled eyes gaze upon Thee all the days of my earthly pilgrimage. Then shall I be prepared to behold Thee in full splendor in the day when Thou shalt appear to be glorified in Thy saints and admired in all them that believe.

—A.W. Tozer

Come! Spirit of Love!

Come! Spirit of Love! Penetrate and transform us by the action of Your purifying life. May Your constant brooding love bring forth in us more love and all the graces and works of love. Give us grace to remain still under its action, and may that humble stillness be our prayer. Amen.

—Evelyn Underhill

A Prayer for Transformation

I pursue You, Jesus, so that I may be caught by You.
I press in so that I may know Your heart.
I stay close so that I may be like You. Loving Lord, grant me:
Purity of heart,
Humility of soul,
Integrity of life,
Charity for all. Amen.

—Richard Foster

Lord Jesus, I Long

Lord Jesus, I long to be perfectly whole,
I want thee forever to live in my soul;
Break down every idol, cast out every foe,
Now wash me, and I shall be whiter than snow.
Lord Jesus, let nothing unholy remain,
Apply Thine own blood and remove every stain;
To get this blest washing I all things forgo;
Now wash me, and I shall be whiter than snow.

—James Nicholson, *The Salvation Army Songbook* 436

All Shall Be Well

In her *Showings*, a discussion of 16 revelations given to her by God, Lady Julian of Norwich says that God, in tender love, comforts all those trapped in pain and sin by speaking these words over them: "But all shall be well, and all shall be well, and all manner of thing shall be well."

Prayers as We Look Outward

These prayers focus upon ministry to others. As you reflect on the compassionate ministry of Jesus, who wept with the sorrowful and laughed with the joyful, pray for the grace to always follow God's way.

May I See You Today

Dearest Lord, may I see You today and every day in the person of Your sick, and, while nursing them, minister unto You. Though You hide Yourself behind the unattractive disguise of the irritable, the exacting, the unreasonable, may I still recognize You, and say: "Jesus, my patient, how sweet it is to serve you."

—Mother Teresa of Calcutta

Open Wide the Windows of our Spirits

Open wide the window of our spirits, O Lord,
And fill us full of light;
Open wide the door of our hearts,
That we may receive and entertain Thee with all our powers
Of adoration and love. Amen.

—Christina G. Rossetti

Enter My Small Life

Lord! Give me courage and love to open the door and constrain You to enter, whatever the disguise You come in, even before I fully recognize my guest. Come in! Enter my small life! Lay your sacred hands on all the common things and small interests of that life and bless and change them. Transfigure my small resources, make them sacred. And in them give me your very Self. Amen.

—Evelyn Underhill

To Do Some Work of Peace for Thee

O Lord, open my eyes that I may see the needs of others;
Open my ears that I may hear their cries;
Open my heart so that they need not be without succor;
Let me not be afraid to defend the weak because of the anger of the strong,

Nor afraid to defend the poor because of the anger of the rich. Show me where love and hope and faith are needed, and use me to bring them to those places. And so open my eyes and my ears that I may this coming day be able to do some work of peace for Thee. Amen.

—Alan Paton

Make Me an Instrument of Thy Peace
Lord, make me an instrument of Thy peace;
Where there is hatred, let me sow love;
Where there is injury, pardon,
Where there is doubt, faith;
Where there is despair, hope;
Where there is darkness, light;
And where there is sadness, joy.
O Divine Master,
Grant that I may not so much seek
To be consoled as to console;
To be understood, as to understand;
To be loved, as to love;
For it is in giving that we receive,
It is in pardoning that we are pardoned,
And it is in dying that we are born to eternal life.

—Francis of Assisi

Here at the Cross
How can I better serve Thee, Lord,
Thou who hast done so much for me?
Faltering and weak my labor has been;
O that my life may tell for Thee!
Here at the cross in this sacred hour,
Here at the source of reviving power
Helpless indeed, I come with my need;
Lord, for Thy service, fit me I plead.

—Bramwell Coles, *The Salvation Army Songbook* 488

CREST BOOKS
(The Salvation Army National Headquarters, Alexandria, VA.)

Shaw Clifton, *Never the Same Again: Encouragement for new and not-so-new Christians*, 1997

Compilation, *Christmas Through the Years: A War Cry Treasury*, 1997

William Francis, *Celebrate the Feasts of the Lord: The Christian Heritage of the Sacred Jewish Festivals*, 1998

Marlene Chase, *Pictures from the Word*, 1998

Joe Noland, *A Little Greatness*, 1998

Lyell M. Rader, *Romance & Dynamite: Essays on Science & the Nature of Faith*, 1998

Shaw Clifton, *Who Are These Salvationists? An Analysis for the 21st Century*, 1999

Compilation, *Easter Through the Years: A War Cry Treasury*, 1999

Terry Camsey, *Slightly Off Center! Growth Principles to Thaw Frozen Paradigms*, 2000

Philip Needham, *He Who Laughed First: Delighting in a Holy God*, (in collaboration with Beacon Hill Press, Kansas City), 2000

Henry Gariepy, ed., *A Salvationist Treasury: 365 Devotional Meditations from the Classics to the Contemporary*, 2000

Marlene Chase, *Our God Comes: And Will Not Be Silent*, 2001

A. Kenneth Wilson, *Fractured Parables: And Other Tales to Lighten the Heart and Quicken the Spirit*, 2001

Carroll Ferguson Hunt, *If Two Shall Agree* (in collaboration with Beacon Hill Press, Kansas City), 2001

John C. Izzard, *Pen of Flame: The Life and Poetry of Catherine Baird*, 2002

Henry Gariepy, *Andy Miller: A Legend and a Legacy*, 2002

Compilation, *A Word in Season: A Collection of Short Stories*, 2002

R. David Rightmire, *Sanctified Sanity: The Life and Teaching of Samuel Logan Brengle*, 2003

Chick Yuill, *Leadership on the Axis of Change*, 2003

Compilation, *Living Portraits Speaking Still: A Collection of Bible Studies*, 2004

A. Kenneth Wilson, *The First Dysfunctional Family: A Modern Guide to the Book of Genesis*, 2004

Allen Satterlee, *Turning Points: How The Salvation Army Found a Different Path*, 2004

David Laeger, *Shadow and Substance: The Tabernacle of the Human Heart*, 2005

Check Yee, *Good Morning China*, 2005

Marlene Chase, *Beside Still Waters: Great Prayers of the Bible for Today*, 2005

Join the Army's network for insight and inspiration

and get a striking color poster showing we are "wonderfully made."

"For You created my inmost being; You knit me together in my
mother's womb. I praise You because I am fearfully and wonderfully made.
My frame was not hidden from You when I was made in the secret place. When
I was woven together in the depths of the earth, Your eyes saw my unformed body.
All the days ordained for me were written in Your book before one of them came to be."
(Ps. 139:13–16)

The National Publications department of The Salvation Army looks forward to supplying you with material that will encourage and inform you. It's a community you can trust, with resources you can use for purposeful living.

The Salvation Army continues in its mission of gospel proclamation and service to humanity without discrimination. It offers you good news in this fast–paced world so you can gain in wisdom and in practical living.

To get your free poster and gain access to news, views, interviews, inspirational articles and books from a Salvation Army perspective, you can:

•visit www.salvation-us.com

•send a note via email to war_cry.salvationarmy.org

•Fill out the card on this page and return it in an envelope to the address provided.

Publications committed to energizing the mission and ministry of The Salvation Army.

Please include me in the Army's network for insight and inspiration

(You can let us know of your interests by checking any of the following.)

❏ Helpful articles, stories, profiles for adolescents and young adults.
❏ News about the Army at the front–lines of emergency relief and ministry
❏ Articles, stories and profiles to aid in spiritual growth.
❏ Books about The Salvation Army and by Salvationists.
❏ Resources I can use for teaching, outreach and ministry.
❏ In–depth analysis of cutting edge theology from a Salvation Army perspective
❏ Consultation and referral for specific questions, needs and concerns.

Name _____

Address _____

City _____

State_____Zip_____

Email address _____

Return to: Salvation Army National Publications, 615 Slaters Lane, Alexandria, VA, 22314